Syntax

Syntax

An Introduction to Minimalism

Elly van Gelderen
Arizona State University

John Benjamins Publishing Company
Amsterdam / Philadelphia

 The paper used in this publication meets the minimum requirements of the American National Standard for Information Sciences – Permanence of Paper for Printed Library Materials, ANSI z39.48-1984.

DOI 10.1075/z.214

Cataloging-in-Publication Data available from Library of Congress:
LCCN 2017041504 (PRINT) / 2017051536 (E-BOOK)

ISBN 978 90 272 1253 5 (HB) / ISBN 978 90 272 1254 2 (PB)
ISBN 978 90 272 6470 1 (E-BOOK)

John Benjamins Publishing Co. · https://benjamins.com

Table of contents

CHAPTER 9
Conclusion

125

Bibliography

131

APPENDIX
Answers to exercises

135

Index of terms and languages

157

Abbreviations

(not mentioned are (N)P, V(P), P(P), and A(P))

ACC	accusative
ant	anterior
asp	aspect, also in ASPP, Aspect Phrase
C(P)	Complementizer (Phrase)
CI	Conceptional Intentional (Interface)
CL	Classifier
COCA	Corpus of Contemporary American English (http://corpus.byu.edu/coca/)
decl	declarative
def	definite
D(P)	Determiner (Phrase)
E	Event
ECM	Exceptional Case Marking
F	feminine
fin	finite
freq	frequentative
fut	future
gen	generic
hab	habitual
i-	interpretable feature
indef	indefinite
M(P)	Mood (Phrase)
NOM	nominative case
NPI	Negative Polarity Item
Num(P)	Number (Phrase)
OM	Object Marker
P	plural
pass	passive
perf	perfect(ive), also used in PerfP
phi	person and number
pres	present
pro	zero subject of finite verbs
PRO	zero subject of non-finite verbs
progr	progressive, also used in ProgrP
Q	Quantifier
rep	repetitive
S	singular or Speech time
T(P)	Tense (Phrase)
u-	uninterpretable feature
VPISH	VP Internal Subject Hypothesis
1	first person
2	second person
3	third person
#	pragmatically marked
*	ungrammatical

List of tables

List of figures

Preface

This is a textbook on generative syntax. It provides general syntactic background as well as an introduction to ideas from the Minimalist Program, the most recent instantiation of generative syntax. Chapter 1 starts with the general idea behind generative grammar and should be read from a big picture perspective. Chapters 2 and 3 provide some background on lexical and grammatical categories and on basic phrase structure rules. After these introductory chapters, the book covers the clausal spine, the VP, TP, and CP in Chapters 4, 5, and 6, respectively. Chapter 7 is about the DP and Chapter 8 discusses the importance of features. Chapter 9 returns to some of the issues raised in Chapter 1 and summarizes the approach.

If students are already familiar with categories, Chapter 2 can be skipped. For students who want to know about the clausal spine and are less interested in the fine details of feature checking, Chapter 8 can be left out.

The main goal of the book is to enable students to understand the structure of sentences in English. The framework developed can then also be applied to other languages, though not much emphasis will be put on that here, except in Chapter 7. The book represents the structure by means of trees, as is common in generative grammar (although no longer in Chomsky 2013; 2015). A second aim is to explain the generative model and some of the recent updates to it, e.g. the shift from a very rich Universal Grammar to a simpler one. Because much of the material is introductory, I have not given copious references, except in Chapter 1. The information in Chapters 2 and 3 is mostly couched in traditional grammatical terminology. In the other chapters, I have only provided references to some of the major ideas, e.g. the VPISH, the VP-shell, and the DP.

I decided to write this book because most introductory textbooks lack the basic information – here included as Chapters 2 and 3 – or are too technical for the students I have in mind, e.g. Adger's 2003 *Core Syntax*, Hornstein, Nunes & Grohmann's 2005 *Understanding Minimalism*, and van Gelderen's 2013 *Clause Structure*. Carnie's 2011 *Syntax* and Radford's 2009a–b are alternatives but have different areas of focus and do not incorporate current Minimalist ideas. I have introduced a few aspects of the current phase of Minimalism (Chomsky 2015) and present a different view of theta-roles, namely as based in inner aspect. Adger's and Radford's sentences are also often judged as too British by my students. I have used a mixture of corpus examples (marked as such) and made-up ones. The corpus examples liven up the text and are also added if the construction is a little unusual.

Chapters 2 and 3 are based on Chapters 2 and 3 in van Gelderen (2010) and Chapter 4 takes some of the ideas from van Gelderen (2013) but makes the discussion less theoretically focused. Many thanks to Naomi Danton, Terje Lohndal, Kleanthes Grohmann, Ad Foolen, and to the students at Arizona State University taking LIN 514 in the spring of 2016 and of 2017 for being so serious and motivated and for helping me clarify issues.

Elly van Gelderen, Apache Junction, AZ

Chapter 1

Generative Grammar

Keywords: Universal Grammar, I-language, E-language, parameters (syntactic and lexical), merge, minimalism, recursion

In this chapter, I provide some background on the major ideas behind generative grammar and on some of the recent changes in its outlook. Generative Grammar has always emphasized the innate component to the Faculty of Language. In recent years, the focus has shifted from a rich Universal Grammar to innate mechanisms that are part of more general cognitive principles and principles of organic systems.

In Section 1, we'll look at reasons for assuming a Universal Grammar and innate cognitive structure. In Section 2, we'll discuss the 'Principles and Parameters' approach, an intuitively appealing way to account for cross-linguistic differences. Section 3 sketches the basics of a Minimalist approach, the Borer-Chomsky Conjecture, and provides a brief introduction to the 'Problems of Projection' approach to phrase/ clause structure. Section 4 is a conclusion.

This chapter provides a broad picture of the aims of generative syntax. Depending on the reader's familiarity with this area, certain parts of this chapter may be somewhat (too?) abstract. Chapter 2 starts with the basics syntax and the other chapters build on that.

1. Universal Grammar

Chomsky's (1957; 1965) generative model offers an approach to language that is focused on acquisition and the faculty of language as represented in the mind/brain. The answer as to how children acquire language so effortlessly is seen as rooted in Universal Grammar. In this model, the focus is on the mind of the language learner/ user (the competence) and ceases to be on the structures present in the language produced (the performance). Thus, children do not imitate what they hear but come up with their own system; see the difficulties this leads to in Figure 1.1.

Baby Blues

Figure 1.1 The Internal Grammar
Baby Blues: © 1997 Baby Blues Partnership Distributed by King Features Syndicate

The input to language learning is poor, a phenomenon known as the 'poverty of the stimulus'. Children hear parts of sentences, false starts, and so on, but still end up with a grammar in their minds/brains that is not dependent on that input or on correction, as Figure 1.1 also attests to.

Speakers know so much more than what they have evidence for from the input. For instance, speakers of English have never been taught that sentences of the type in (1a) are grammatical but those in (1b) are not. Yet, they know this difference.

(1)   a.   Who did you say **that** you intend to invite?   (adapted COCA fiction 2014)
       b.   *Who did you say **when** you intend to invite?

In (1a), *who* originates as the object of *invite* and is fronted to form the *wh*-question; in (1b), the same happens but somehow changing *that* to *when* makes the sentence ungrammatical. We'll talk about this phenomenon more in Chapter 5; the point here is that we know how to distinguish grammatical sentences from ungrammatical ones, without instruction. Note that prescriptive grammar demands *whom* in (1) but that this accusative form of the *wh*-word is in decline in both spoken and written English.

As a note on the examples sentences, I use made-up examples if they are un-controversial and use corpus examples, e.g. from the Corpus of American English (COCA) in (1a), to convince you that they occur or to liven up the text.

When we look at c-command in Chapter 3, we encounter another example of a phenomenon that depends on principles in the internal grammar rather than on something that is necessary for communicative purposes. So, in (2), the closest ante-cedent to the reflexive pronoun is the feminine *Jane* but the correct form is *himself*, as in (2a), not *herself*. Why couldn't (2b) mean that 'he voted for her'?

(2)   a.   The husband of Jane voted for **himself**.
       b.   *The husband of Jane voted for **herself**.

The parasitic gap in (3) is a construction native speakers of English have never been taught but which they have grammatical judgments on. The gaps in (3), indicated by underlined spaces, show that *which articles* is the object of both the verb *file* and the verb *reading*.

(3)   Which articles did John file __ without reading __?

The interesting property is that *which articles* in (3) is connected to two different gaps – hence the name parasitic gap – and this is usually not grammatical, as (4) shows.

(4)   *Who was he sent a picture of __ to __?
      [meaning: To whom and of whom was he sent a picture?]

How do speakers know that it is grammatical to have an extra, i.e. parasitic, gap in (3) but not in (4)?

How is the acquisition of phenomena such as those in (1) to (4) possible? It is based on impoverished input since native speakers may never actually have heard (1a), (2a), or (3) and still know that they are grammatical. The answer to this problem, 'Plato's Problem' in Chomsky (1986), is Universal Grammar, the initial state of the language faculty. This biologically innate organ helps the learner make sense of the data and build an internal grammar (I-language), which then produces the sentences a speaker utters (E-language). See Figure 1.2.

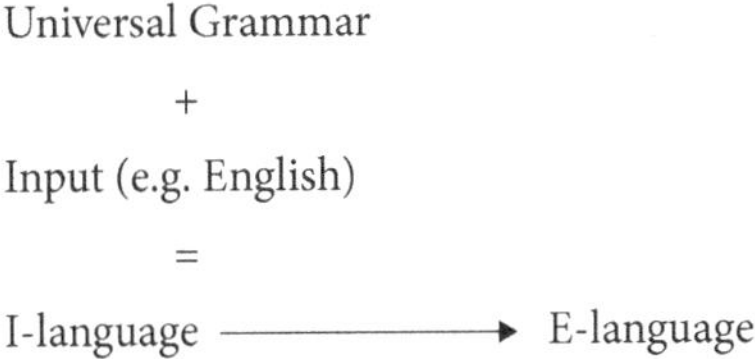

Figure 1.2 Model of language acquisition (initial version)

The innate language faculty, when "stimulated by appropriate and continuing experience, … creates a grammar that creates sentences with formal and semantic properties", according to Chomsky (1975: 36). Thus, our innate language faculty (or Universal Grammar) enables us to create a set of rules, or grammar, by being exposed to (rather chaotic) language around us. This input may be English or any other language. The set of rules that we acquire enables us to produce sentences that we have never heard before and that can be infinitely long (if we have the time and energy).

Language acquisition, in this framework, is not imitation but an interaction between Universal Grammar and exposure to a particular language. "Learning is primarily a matter of filling in detail within a structure that is innate" (Chomsky 1975: 39). "A physical organ, say the heart, may vary from one person to the next in size or strength, but its basic structure and its function within human physiology are common to the species. Analogously, two individuals in the same speech community may acquire grammars that differ somewhat in scale and subtlety. ... These variations in structure are limited ..." (1975: 38).

Universal Grammar of the 1950s to 1970s has a lot of specific instructions and rules. It includes rules for antecedent-reflexive relations to account for (2) and for *wh*-movement to account for (1), (3), and (4). If humans only had 100,000 to 200,000 years – as is currently speculated – to develop the Faculty of Language, it makes sense to attribute less to it. Currently, Universal Grammar just contains a simple operation 'merge' that combines two elements into a set. Merge includes what is referred to in this book as 'move': the merging element is taken from inside the derivation and copied. If Universal Grammar is no longer so important, the pre-linguistic conceptual structure plays a much larger role, as I now show.

In Chapter 4, we'll discuss the VP which is where the information is situated on 'who does what to whom', i.e. the argument structure. Arguments are obligatory elements for verbs. For instance, the verb *arrive* has one argument, *the bus*, in (5a) and *give* has three, *they, us*, and *books*, in (6a). Adding more, as in (5b), or deleting one, as in (6b), renders an ungrammatical sentence.

(5) a. The bus arrived.
     b. * He arrived the bus.

(6) a. They gave us books.
     b. * They gave us.

There is a debate as to how much of this information is listed with the verb in the lexicon (Levin & Rappaport Hovav 1995) and how much added by the syntax (Borer 2005a–b). The big question is how children acquire this structure, which is very complex. For instance, we distinguish arguments that are Agents from those that are Themes and various researchers show that children distinguish intransitive verbs with Agents (*swim*) from those with Themes (*fall*) from the moment they start using these verbs (e.g. Snyder, Hyams & Crisma 1995; Costa & Friedmann 2012, and Ryan 2012). That implies these concepts are innate. Children also distinguish the aspectual manner from result verbs by using *-ing* in English for the former and past tense *-ed* for the latter. We'll talk about Agents, Themes, and aspect more in Chapter 4.

Bickerton (1990: 67) sees "[a]rgument structure ... [a]s universal." He writes that the "universality of thematic structure suggests a deep-rooted ancestry, perhaps one lying outside language altogether" (1990: 185). All languages have verbs for eating and drinking and those verbs would have an Agent and a Theme connected with them. Arguments are also represented in the syntax in predictable ways. Jackendoff (2002), based on Bickerton, suggests that pre-linguistic primate conceptual structure may already use symbols for basic semantic relations. If argument/thematic structure predates the emergence of language, an understanding of causation, intentionality, volition – all relevant to determining Agents, Causers, and Themes – may be part of our larger cognitive system and not restricted to the language faculty.

Chomsky's main interest is not the cognitive structure but the syntax and he devotes only a few words to the acquisition of the lexical knowledge. Early on (1965: 142), he says that "semantic features ... too, are presumably drawn from a universal 'alphabet' but little is known about this today and nothing has been said about it here." This tradition of assuming innate knowledge goes back to the Greeks. A French source from the 17th century says the following about ideas:

> Ils "ne tirent en aucune sorte leur origine des sens. Notre âme a la faculté de les former de soi-même."
> They 'do not in any fashion have their origin in the senses. Our mind has the faculty to form those on its own.'   (Arnauld & Nicole 1662 [1965]: 45)

In the next section, I'll describe the Principles and Parameters approach to Universal Grammar because it was very influential in the 1980s and 1990s and is still used as a descriptive tool today. Then, I show how it is seen now, namely as restricted to the lexicon.

2.   Parameters: From syntax to lexicon

In the 1980s and 1990s, parameters are seen as choices that Universal Grammar makes available to the language learner. They have to be set as +/– on the basis of the available linguistic evidence. Early examples of parameters that Universal Grammar is seen to supply are pro-drop (Rizzi 1982), headedness (Stowell 1981), and movement of *wh*-elements (Huang 1982).

Pro-drop is the cover term for a set of related phenomena, the absence of the subject of a finite verb, the possibility to have subject-inversion, and more (see Chomsky 1981: 240). Not many linguists, however, believe that the phenomenon involves a +/– setting of an actual parameter called 'pro-drop' and now it is seen as a property of the lexicon, as I'll mention later on.

If a transitive verb has no subject or object, these arguments are nevertheless assumed to be present because otherwise the verb does not have its regular meaning. So, the meaning of *go* depends on someone going. The empty subjects are usually referred to with the first three letters of the word 'pronoun'. If the empty subject is the subject of a non-finite verb, we refer to it as PRO ('big PRO'), as in (7).

(7)   **pronounced as:**
   I want PRO to go.   I want to go. / I wanna go.

If it is the subject of a finite verb, as in (8), we refer to it as pro ('little pro'). (8) is the Spanish translation of (7) that shows Spanish has both pro and PRO.

(8)   **pronounced as:**
   pro quiero PRO venir.   Quiero venir.

Modern English has PRO but not pro, since a tensed/finite clause cannot have a null subject, as (9) shows.

(9) *Now pro am talking to myself.   Now am talking to myself.

Some criteria for distinguishing between PRO and pro are that PRO is obligatorily empty, while pro is optionally so, and that PRO is universally available if languages have the appropriate non-finite clauses but pro exists only in certain languages. When we talk about the Pro-drop parameter, we mean small pro.

In short, Modern English has null or empty subjects with infinitives, as in (7), but lacks unexpressed subjects with finite sentences, as (9) shows. Spanish has both PRO and pro and is therefore a pro-drop language. There are other kinds of empty elements or copies. Thus, if an element moves, it leaves a copy, as *who* does in (1), and all languages have these elements. (Copies are sometimes referred to as traces).

Headedness is a helpful way to characterize a language, with Arabic, Irish, and Chinese being head-initial and Japanese, Hindi/Urdu, and Korean head-final. Verbs, prepositions, and nouns precede their complements in head-initial languages but follow them in head-final ones. Examples are given in (10) and (11).

(10) a. *wo he   cha*   Chinese VO
     1s drink tea
     'I drink tea.' (tense is not marked here)

   b. *gen ta*   Chinese PO
     with 3s
     'with her/him'

(11) a. *Mẽ kitaab perhti hũ.*   Hindi/Urdu OV
     1s book   read be.1s
     'I am reading the book.' (I am ignoring the feminine on *perhti*)

   b. *mez per*   Hindi/Urdu PO
     table on
     'on the table'

Languages can also be head-initial for the P and head-final for the V, or have another combination of category-specific headedness. Kayne (1994) abandons headedness and argues that SVO is basic; other word orders come about through movement. This position is frequently followed but one still encounters work using V-final as basic and, as we'll see in Section 3, recent work that says the syntax is unordered.

The *wh*-movement parameter describes the variation languages show in whether they move the *wh*-pronoun or not, as in (12).

(12)   *ni xiangxin ta hui shuo **shenme***   Chinese
        2s think   3s will say what
        'What do you think s/he will say?'

Though most introductory generative syntax books (Radford 2009a–b) continue to cite this set of syntactic parameters, *pro*-drop/null subject, headedness, and *wh*-movement, these are often used in very descriptive ways, not to explain what goes on in language acquisition. Since Chomsky (1995), a major question is how these parameters would have arisen in the brain. If the shift in humans from no language to language was immediate, it makes sense that there is one crucial change in the way the brain functions and that change could have been the introduction of merge. Complex parameters of the *pro*-drop variety don't fit in this non-gradual picture of evolution.

In addition, especially since Borer (1984), parameters have come to be seen as choices of feature specifications as the child acquires a lexicon (Chomsky 2007). To account for pro-drop, we assume that the Spanish lexicon includes an item with just person and number features but no phonology. The computational system of every language is seen as the same but the parametric choices are lexical and account for the variety of languages. They also determine linear order but have no effect on the semantic component. Baker, while disagreeing with this view of parameters, calls this the Borer-Chomsky-Conjecture.

(13)   **Borer-Chomsky-Conjecture**
      "All parameters of variation are attributable to differences in the features of
      particular items (e.g., the functional heads) in the lexicon."   (Baker 2008: 156)

The conjecture in (13) describes how the lexicon is acquired. Children need to combine the various (innate) semantic features into words.

Section 2 has outlined three traditional parameters that used to be seen as part of Universal Grammar. They no longer are seen this way but nevertheless are helpful in describing differences between languages.

3.   Minimalism

In this section, I discuss what Minimalism is, how it shifted from a focus on Universal Grammar to third factor principles, and what the most recent instantiation looks like.

Minimalism is a program, not a theory, as Chomsky always emphasizes. It encourages inquiry into certain questions, such as 'why is language the way it is'? The computational system is assumed to contain only what is necessary to build representations that connect sound (or sign or writing) to meaning. It is the same for all languages. Because of this line of inquiry, derivations and structural representations have become extremely bare, as we'll see at the end of this section.

Since Chomsky (2005; 2007), as mentioned, the emphasis is on innate principles not specific to the language faculty (Universal Grammar), but to "general properties of organic systems" (Chomsky 2004: 105). Chomsky identifies the three factors that are crucial in the development of language as follows, where I have taken the most explicit formulations from different publications.

Three Factors

1. Genetic endowment, apparently nearly uniform for the species, which interprets part of the environment as linguistic experience, a nontrivial task that the infant carries out reflexively, and which determines the general course of the development of the language faculty. Among the genetic elements, some may impose computational limitations that disappear in a regular way through genetically timed maturation …;
2. Experience, which leads to variation, within a fairly narrow range, as in the case of other subsystems of the human capacity and the organism generally" (Chomsky 2005: 6);
3. Principles not specific to FL [the Faculty of Language]. Some of the third factor principles have the flavor of the constraints that enter into all facets of growth and evolution …. Among these are principles of efficient computation". (Chomsky 2007: 3)

The first factor is the traditional Universal Grammar and the second factor is the experience that we saw in Figure 1.1. The third factor is new but somewhat related to the first; it is favored above the language-specific one (for reasons of simplicity). The third factor can be divided into several types, including principles of efficient computation. Economy Principles are probably also part of more general cognitive principles, thus reducing the role of Universal Grammar even more. Figure 1.2 can therefore be adapted as Figure 1.3.

Universal Grammar, cognitive principles, and third factors

$+$

Input (e.g. English)

$=$

I-language ⟶ E-language

Figure 1.3 Model of language acquisition (final version)

As mentioned, the Minimalist Program proposes syntactic models and derivations that are very minimal and the same for every language. Interfacing with the syntactic derivation are the Conceptual-Intentional and Sensory-Motor systems. The former is responsible for providing an interpretation and includes non-linguistic knowledge where the latter is responsible for externalizing the derivation i.e. providing a spoken or signed or written representation.

The minimalist model for deriving a sentence from 1995 on involves making a selection from the lexicon, as in (14), and merging these items together, as in (15), from bottom to top. The brackets indicate unordered sets that need to be ordered when they are externalized.

(14)   {they, read, will, the, books}

(15)   a.   {the, books}
       b.   {read, {the, books}}
       c.   {they, {read, {the, books}}}
       d.   {will, {they, {read, {the, books}}}}
       e.   {they, {will, {~~they~~, {read, {the, books}}}}}

In steps (15a–b), we are just combining the object and the verb, i.e. constructing the VP. The other steps depend on the subject of the sentence being merged immediately with the VP (15c) before the auxiliary *will* is in (15d). Sometimes the merge is 'internal', from inside the derivation, e.g. *they* in (15e). We often refer to this as the subject moving to a higher position. We'll talk about the details in Chapters 4 and 5.

In this book, as in e.g. Kayne (1994; 2013), we will not follow Chomsky in having an unordered derivation. We will argue there is a base order, SVO, with an Agent before the Verb and its Theme. The reason for this is that the externalization is not understood well if we have a derivation without order, as in (15).

Another way of representing the derivation in (15) is through a tree, as in (16), which I have only partially filled in. The TP is the Tense Phrase, where all vital information on finiteness and agreement is stored. We will assume that what appears to the left of one word in the tree will also be spoken, signed, or written first.

(16)

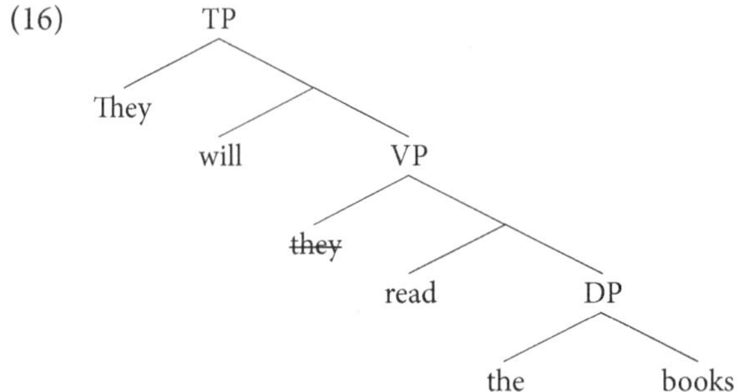

Merge as in (15) and (16) is recursive; one can continue to merge if there is enough time. This property means we can make sentences that are in principle endless, as in (17).

(17)   I thought she mentioned that they were leaving because they had to visit an uncle who was now living abroad in order to …

The current Problems of Projection (PoP) approach within Minimalism insists that the derivation in (16) isn't labelled when the tree/derivation is built. It says that syntax only combines objects and yields unordered sets {X, Y} without a label (Chomsky 2013: 42), as already shown in (15). The labeling is done when the syntax hands over its combined sets to the interfaces, as shown in Figure 1.4, which represents the current model. This labeling mechanism is a third factor principle: needed for the interfaces.

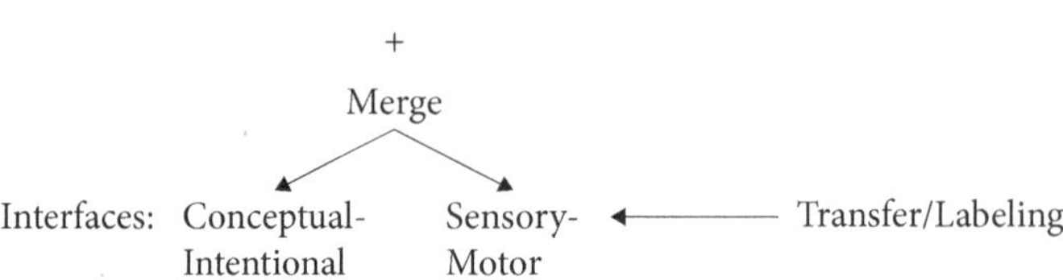

Figure 1.4 The Minimalist model of language generation

Attractive in this model is that movement, as we'll see is frequent in Chapters 4 and 5, is "driven by labeling failures" (Chomsky 2015: 7). For instance, if two phrases are merged together, their heads are both as accessible and could both label the result. This is a paradox that is resolved when one of the two moves and provides an explanation for the movement of the subject that we'll see in Chapter 4.

The PoP approach is still being debated and, even if it is accepted that the syntax doesn't label phrases, we still need to know the structure of sentences and the order in which the words are externalized. Therefore, we will continue to use labeled and ordered trees in the chapters that follow.

4.   Conclusion

In this chapter, I have introduced Universal Grammar, innate structure, parameters, merge, and labeling. Some of this will sound very abstract at this stage but I wanted to give an indication of where the generative syntactic model is going. Mentioning the unlabeled trees should make you worry less about all the fine details; we'll put the details in (most of the time) but that may be for descriptive purposes. Differences between languages arise through lexical choices learners make in building the lexicon of a particular language: pronouns may vary between full phrases or heads and the inflection may be elaborate or not.

At the end of this chapter, you should be able to give an example of a traditional syntactic parameter and know a little about the role of Universal Grammar in the Minimalist Program. In the exercises, we'll practice how to do glosses that we've seen in (10) to (12) and (14) and (15), and to analyze example sentences from languages other than (Modern) English.

Exercises

A.   Radford (2009b: 35) provides the following sentence from Lucy. Descriptively speaking, when Lucy produces (1), what is she doing? Which parameters have been set?

(1)   What doing? (meaning: What are you doing?)

B.   Using the list of abbreviations in the front of this book, what is the word order in (2), head-initial or head-final? How would you translate this Hopi sentence (from Kalectaca 1978)?

(2)   *Nu' kwaahu-t tuwa.*
       1s   eagle-OM saw

C.   We will use two kinds of glosses for other languages: a morpheme-by-morpheme gloss, using abbreviated symbols, and a freer translation, enclosed in single quotation marks. Both are not always provided if the meaning is clear. The glosses list morphological features such as accusative (acc) in cases where this is relevant for our discussion. Hyphens are used when we can clearly see the morphemes; periods indicate morphemes that are fused. Much stricter glosses are suggested at <www.eva.mpg.de/lingua/resources/glossing-rules.php> Knowing this, explain in words what the glosses in (3) mean.

(3)   *mẽ   kahaanii likh-tii   hũ.*   Urdu/Hindi 20th century
       1S.NOM(F) story   write-PRES.F be.PRES.1S
       'I am writing a story.'

D.   Find a language of your own choice and explore if it has pro-drop.

E.   Which special characteristic of the faculty of language is shown in Figure 1.5?

Figure 1.5 "I'm telling on you" <http://babyblues.com/comics/march-19-2007>
Baby Blues: © 2007 Baby Blues Partnership Distributed by King Features Syndicate

F.   To get some practice with corpus examples, find an example with a reflexive pronoun in COCA and one in the BNC <http://corpus.byu.edu/bnc>

Chapter 2

Building blocks

Keywords: Lexical and grammatical categories (N, V, A, P, D, T, C), finiteness, case, agreement, types of auxiliaries, pronouns

This chapter reviews the lexical and grammatical categories of English and provides criteria on how to decide whether a word is, for example, a noun or an adjective or a demonstrative. This knowledge of categories, also known as parts of speech, can then be applied to languages other than English. The chapter also examines pronouns, which have grammatical content but may function like nouns, and looks at how categories change.

Categories continue to be much discussed. Some linguists argue that the mental lexicon lists no categories, just roots without categorial information, and that morphological markers (e.g. *-ion, -en,* and zero) make roots into categories. I will assume there are categories of two kinds, lexical and grammatical. This distinction between lexical and grammatical is relevant to a number of phenomena that are listed in Table 2.1. For instance, lexical categories are learned early, can be translated easily, and be borrowed because they have real meaning; grammatical categories do not have lexical meaning, are rarely borrowed, and may lack stress. Switching between languages (code switching) is easier for lexical than for grammatical categories.

Table 2.1 The practical use of a distinction between lexical and grammatical categories

Lexical	Grammatical
First Language Acquisition starts with lexical categories, e.g. *Mommy eat.*	Borrowed grammatical categories are rare: the prepositions *per, via,* and *plus* are the rare borrowings.
Lexical categories can be translated into another language easily.	Grammatical categories contract and may lack stress, e.g. *He's going* for *he is going.*
Borrowed words are mainly lexical, e.g. *taco, sudoko, Zeitgeist.*	Code switching between grammatical categories is hard:
Code switching occurs: I saw *adelaars*	* *Ik am talking to the neighbors.*
(English Dutch) eagles	I (Dutch – English)

Traditional parts of speech are noun, pronoun, adjective, determiner, verb, adverb, preposition, conjunction, and interjection. This use is meant in the question in Figure 2.1.

Figure 2.1 Parts of speech
Family Circus: © 2004 Bil Keane, Inc. Distributed by King Features Syndicate, Inc.

We'll divide the parts of speech into three groups and ignore the interjections since they can be of any category.

The outline of this chapter is as follows. In Section 1, we examine the lexical categories, N, V, A, and P. The grammatical categories D, T, and C are discussed in Section 2. Section 3 treats pronouns separately because they have a little of both categories. Finally, Section 4 gives a brief overview of the chapter.

1.   Lexical categories

The five lexical categories in English are Noun, Verb, Adjective, Adverb, and Preposition. They carry meaning and words with a similar (synonym) or opposite meaning (antonym) can often be found. Frequently, the noun is said to be a person, place, or thing and the verb is said to be an event or act. These are semantic definitions. Semantic definitions are not completely adequate and we'll need to define categories syntactically (according to what they combine with) and morphologically (according to how the words are formed).

As just mentioned, a noun generally indicates a person, place or thing (i.e. this is its meaning). For instance, *chair, table*, and *book* are nouns since they refer to things.

However, if the distinction between a noun as person, place, or thing and a verb as an event or action were the only distinction, certain nouns such as *action* and *destruction* would be verbs, since they imply action. These elements are nevertheless nouns because of their syntactic behavior and morphological shape. In (1) and (2), *actions* and *destruction* are preceded by the article *the*, *actions* can be made singular by taking the plural *-s* off, and *destruction* can be pluralized with an *-s*. That makes them nouns.

(1)   The **actions** by the government helped a lot.

(2)   The earthquake caused the **destruction** of that city.

Apart from plural *-s*, other morphological characteristics of nouns are shown in (3) and (4). Possessive *'s* (or genitive case) appears only on nouns, e.g. the noun *Emily* in (3), and affixes such as *-er* and *-ism*, e.g. *writer* and *postmodernism* in (4), are also typical for nouns.

(3)   **Emily's** uncle always knows the answer.

(4)   That **writer** has destroyed **postmodernism.**

Syntactic reasons for calling certain words nouns are that nouns are often preceded by *the*, as *actions* and *government* are in (1), as *destruction* is in (2), and as *answer* is in (3). Nouns can also be preceded by the demonstrative *that*, as in (2) and (4), and, if they are followed by another noun, there has to be a preposition, such as *by* in (1) and *of* in (2), connecting them.

The nouns *action* and *destruction* have verbal counterparts, namely *act* and *destroy*, shown in (5) and (6) respectively.

(5)   The government **acted** too late.

(6)   The earthquake **destroyed** the villages.

Just as nouns cannot always be defined as people or things, verbs are not always acts, even though *acted* and *destroyed* are. The verb *be* in (7), represented by the third person present form *is*, does not express an action. Hence, we need to add state to the semantic definition of verb, as well as emotion to account for sentences such as (8).

(7)   The story **is** interesting.

(8)   The memoir **seemed** nice (to me).

Some of the morphological characteristics of verbs are that they can express tense, e.g. past tense ending *-ed* in (5), (6), and (8); that the verb ends in *-s* when it has a third person singular subject and is present tense; and that it may have an affix typical for verbs, namely *-ize*, e.g. in *modernized* in (4) (note that it is *-ise* in British English). Syntactically, they can be followed by a noun, as in (6), as well as by a preposition and they can be preceded by an auxiliary, as in (4). Some of the major differences between nouns and verbs are summarized in Table 2.2 below.

In English, nouns can easily be used as verbs and verbs as nouns. Therefore, it is necessary to look at the context in which a word occurs, as in (9), for example, where Shakespeare uses *vnckle*, i.e. 'uncle', as a verb as well as a noun.

(9)   York: Grace me no Grace, nor **Vnckle** me,
      I am no Traytors **Vnckle**; and that word Grace
      In an vngracious mouth, is but prophane.
                      (Shakespeare, *Richard II*, II, 3, 96, as in the First Folio edition)

Thus, using the criteria discussed above, the first instance of 'uncle' would be a verb since the noun following it does not need to be connected to the verb by means of a preposition, and the second 'uncle' is a noun since 'traitor' has the possessive *'s*. Note that I have left Shakespeare's spelling, punctuation, and grammar as they appear in the First Folio Edition. I follow the original spelling in other examples as well.

Other examples where a word can be both a noun and a verb are *table, to table; chair, to chair; floor, to floor; book, to book; fax, to fax; telephone, to telephone;* and *walk, to walk.* Some of these started out (historically) as nouns and some as verbs. For instance, *fax* is the shortened form of the noun *facsimile* which became used as a verb as well; *pdf* (portable document format) is another noun that is now used as a verb. A sentence where *police* is used as noun, verb, and adjective respectively is (10a); (10b) is nicely alliterating where *pickle* is used as a verb, adjective, and noun; and (10c) has *fast* as adjective, adverb, and noun.

(10)   a.   **Police police police** outings regularly in the meadows of Malacandra.
       b.   Did Peter Piper **pickle pickled pickles?**   (Alyssa Bachman's example)
       c.   The **fast** girl recovered **fast** after her **fast.**   (Amy Shinabarger's example)

As a summary, I provide a table. Not all of these properties are always present of course. Morphological differences (a to c; h to j) involve the shape of an element while syntactic ones (d to f: k to m) involve how the element fits in a sentence. The semantic differences (g and n) involve meaning, but remember to be careful here since nouns, for instance, can have verbal meanings as in (1) and (2) above.

Table 2.2 Some differences between N(oun) and V(erb)

		Noun (N)		Verb (V)
Morphology	a.	plural *-s* with a few exceptions, e.g. *children, deer, mice*	h.	past tense *-ed* with a few exceptions, e.g. *went, left*
	b.	possessive *'s*	i.	third person singular agreement *-s*
	c.	some end in *-ity, -ness -ation, -er, -ion, -ment*	j.	some end in *-ize, -ate*
Syntax	d.	may follow *the/a* and *this/that/these/those*	k.	may follow an auxiliary e.g. *have* and *will*
	e.	modified by adjective	l.	modified by adverb
	f	followed by preposition and noun	m.	followed by noun or preposition and noun
Semantics	g.	person, place, thing	n.	act, event, state, emotion

Differences (e) and (l) are evident in (11), which shows the adjective *expensive* that modifies (i.e. says something about) the noun *book* and the adverb *quickly* that modifies the verb *sold out*.

(11)   That **expensive** book sold out **quickly**.

Adverbs and Adjectives are semantically very similar in that both modify another element, i.e. they describe a quality of another word: *quick/ly, nice/ly*, etc. The main syntactic distinction is as expressed in (12).

(12)   **The Adjective-Adverb Rule**
An adjective modifies a noun;
an adverb modifies a verb and a degree adverb modifies an adjective or adverb.

Since an adjective modifies a noun, the quality it describes will be one appropriate to a noun, e.g. nationality/ethnicity (*American, Navajo, Dutch, Iranian*), size (*big, large, thin*), age (*young, old*), color (*red, yellow, blue*), material/personal description (*wooden, human*), or character trait (*happy, fortunate, lovely, pleasant, obnoxious*). Some instances of the use of the adjective *nice* are given in (13) and (14). Traditionally, the use in (13) is called predicative and that in (14) attributive.

(13)   The book is **interesting.**

(14)   An **interesting** book is on the table.

Adverbs often modify actions and will then provide information typical of those, e.g. manner (*wisely, fast, quickly, slowly*), as in (11), or duration (*frequently, often*), or speaker attitude (*fortunately, actually*), or place (*there, abroad*), or time (*then, now, yesterday*). *As well* and *also*, and negatives such as *not* and *never*, are also adverbs in that they usually modify the verb. When adverbs modify adjectives or other adverbs, they are called degree adverbs (*very, so, too*). These degree adverbs have very little meaning (except some that can add flavor to the degree, such as *exceedingly* and *amazingly*) and it is hard to find synonyms or antonyms. It therefore makes more sense to consider this subgroup of adverbs grammatical categories. They also do not head a phrase of their own, and when it looks as if they do, there really is another adjective or adverb left out. The *very* in (15) modifies *important*, which is left out.

(15)   How important is your job to you? **Very.**   (from CBS 60 Minutes 1995)

The adverbs *very* and *quickly* appear in (16) and (17).

(16)   This Zuni figurine is **very** precious.

(17)   They drove **very quickly.**

In (13) and (14), *interesting* modifies the noun *book*. In (15), the degree adverb *very* modifies the adjective *precious*; and in (17), it modifies the adverb *quickly*, which in its turn modifies the verb *drove*.

Sentence (16) shows something else, namely that the noun *Zuni* can also be used to modify another noun. When words are put together like this, they are called compound words. Other examples are given in (18) and (19).

(18)   So the principal says to the [**chemistry** teacher], "You'll have to teach physics this year."   (COCA Science Activities 1990)

(19)   Relaxing in the living room of his unpretentious red [**stone** house], ...
          (COCA Forbes 1990)

Some of these compounds may end up being seen or written as one word, e.g. *girlfriend, bookmark, mail-carrier, fire engine, dog food*, and *stone age*. When we see a noun modifying another noun, as in (18) and (19), they can be compounds. A compound has a distinct stress pattern from two words: try pronouncing 'a greenhouse' and 'a green house'. The space and hyphen between the two words indicate degrees of closeness.

Often, an adverb is formed from an adjective by adding *-ly*, as in (17). However, be careful with this morphological distinction: not all adverbs end in *-ly*, e.g., *fast, hard*, and *low*, whereas some adjectives end in *-ly*, e.g. *friendly, lovely, lively*, and *wobbly*. Check to see what it modifies in a sentence, using rule (12). For instance, in (20), *fast* is an adjective because it modifies the noun *car*, but in (21), it is an adverb since it modifies the verb *drove*.

(20)   That **fast** car must be a police car.

(21)   That car drove **fast** until it hit the photo radar.

In a number of cases, words such as *hard* and *fast* can be adjectives or adverbs, depending on the interpretation. In (22), *hard* can either modify the noun *person*, i.e. the person looks tough or nasty, in which case it is an adjective, or it can modify *look* (meaning that the person was looking all over the place for something, i.e. the effort was great) in which case *hard* is an adverb.

(22)   That person looked **hard.**

Some of the 'discrepancies' between form and function are caused by language change. For instance, the degree adverb *very* started out its life being borrowed as an adjective from the French *verrai* (in the 13th century) with the meaning 'true', as in (23).

(23)   *Under the colour of a* **veray** *peax, whiche is neuertheles but a cloked and furred peax.*
'Under the color of a true peace, which is nevertheless nothing but a cloaked and furred peace.'   (Cromwell's 16th century Letters)

Here, what looks like a *-y* ending is a rendering of the Old French *verrai*. In Old English, adverbs do not need to end in *-lich* or *-ly*. That's why 'old' adverbs sometimes keep that shape, e.g. *first* in (24) is a 'correct' adverb, but *second* is not. The reason that *secondly* is prescribed rather than *second* is that it was borrowed late from French, when English adverbs typically received *-ly* endings.

(24)   ... **first** I had to watch the accounts and **secondly** I'm looking at all this stuff for when I start my business.   (from a conversation in the BNC Corpus)

A last point to make about adjectives and adverbs is that most (if they are gradable) can be used to compare or contrast two or more things. We call such forms the comparative (e.g. *better than*) or superlative (e.g. *the best*). One way to make these forms is to add *-er/-est*, as in *nicer/nicest*. Not all adjectives/adverbs allow this ending, however; some need to be preceded by *more/most*, as in *more intelligent, most intelligent*. Sometimes, people are creative with comparatives and superlatives, especially in advertising, as in (25) and (26), or in earlier forms as in (27).

(25)   mechanic: "the **expensivest** oil is ..."

(26)   advertisement: "the **bestest** best ever phone".

(27)   To take the **basest** and **most poorest** shape ...   (Shakespeare, *King Lear* II, 3, 7)

There are also irregular comparative and superlative forms, such as *good, better, best; bad, worse, worst*. These have to be learned as exceptions to the rules, and can be played with, as in the pun 'When I am bad, I am better'.

To summarize, the table below lists differences between adjectives and adverbs. Not all of these differences have been discussed yet, e.g. the endings *-ous, -ary, -al,* and *-ic* are typical for adjectives and *-wise*, and *-ways* for adverbs, but they speak for themselves.

Table 2.3 Differences between adjectives and adverbs

		Adjectives (Adj)		Adverbs (Adv)
Morphology	a.	end in *-ous, -ary, -al, -ic*; mostly have no *-ly*; and can be participles	d.	end in *-ly* in many cases, *-wise*, *-ways*, etc. or have no ending (*fast, now*)
Syntax	b.	modify N	e.	modify V, Adj, or Adv
Semantics	c.	describe qualities typical of nouns, e.g: nationality, color, size.	f.	describe qualities of verbs, e.g: place, manner, time, duration, etc. and degree in adjectives/ adverbs

Prepositions typically express place or time (*at, in, on, before*), direction (*to, from, into, down*), causation (*for*), or relation (*of, about, with, like, as, near*). They are invariable in form and have to occur before a noun, as (28) shows, where the prepositions are in bold and the nouns they go with are underlined.

(28)   **With** their <u>notes</u> **about** <u>biology</u>, they went **to** <u>the woods</u>.

On occasion, what look like prepositions are used on their own, as in (29).

(29)   He went **in**; they ran **out**; and he jumped **down**.

In such cases, these words are considered adverbs, not prepositions. The difference between prepositions and adverbs is that prepositions come before the nouns they relate to and that adverbs are on their own, modifying something but movable.

Some other examples of one word prepositions are *during, around, after, against, despite, except, without, towards, until, till,* and *inside*. Sequences such as *instead of, outside of, away from, due to,* and *as for* are also considered to be prepositions, even though they consist of more than one word. Infrequently, prepositions are transformed into verbs, as in (30).

(30)   They **upped** the price.

Some prepositions have very little lexical meaning and are mainly used for grammatical purposes. For instance, *of* in (31) expresses a relationship between two nouns rather than a locational or directional meaning.

(31)   The door **of** that car.

Prepositions are therefore a category with lexical and grammatical characteristics. Here, however, I will treat them as lexical, for the sake of simplicity. A partial list is given in Table 2.4.

Table 2.4 Some prepositions in English

about, above, across, after, against, along, amidst, among, around, at, before, behind, below, beneath, beside(s), between, beyond, by, concerning, despite, down, during, except, for, from, in, into, inside, like, near, of, off, on, onto, opposite, outside, over, past, since, through, till, to, toward(s), under, underneath, until, up, upon, with, within, without

2. Grammatical Categories

The grammatical categories are Determiner, Auxiliary, Coordinator, and Complementizer. In this chapter and the next, we will use D for all determiners, T (tense) for the auxiliaries – later, we add Asp(ect) and M(ood) – and C for both coordinator and complementizer. It is hard to define grammatical categories in terms of meaning because they have very little. Their function is to make the lexical categories fit together.

The determiner category includes the articles *a(n)* and *the*, as well as demonstratives, possessive pronouns, possessive nouns, some quantifiers, some interrogatives, and some numerals. So, determiner (or D) is an umbrella term for all of these. They will be summarized in Table 2.5. Determiners occur with a noun to specify which noun is meant or whose it is.

The indefinite article is often used when the noun that follows it is new in the text/conversation, such as the first mention of *an elephant* in (32) is. The second mention of *elephant* is preceded by the definite article *the*. Both belong to the category of determiner.

(32)   **An elephant** marched hundreds of kilometres and briefly crossed into Somalia this month marking the first time **the animal** has been seen in the country in 20 years, conservationists said Wednesday.

<http://phys.org/news/2016-03-elephant-somalia-years.html>

There are four demonstratives in English: *this, that, these,* and *those*, with the first two for singular nouns and the last two for plural ones. Sentence (33a) includes a singular and a plural demonstrative. Possessive pronouns include *my, your, his, her, its, our,* and *their*, as in (33b). Nouns can be possessives as well, but in that case they have an *-'s* (or *'*) ending, as in (33c).

(33)   a.   **That** coyote loved **these** trails.
       b.   **Their** kangaroo ate **my** food.
       c.   **Gucci's** food was eaten by Coco.

In (33b), *their* and *my* specify whose kangaroo and whose food it was, and the possessive noun *Gucci's* in (33c) specifies whose food was eaten.

Determiners, as in (32) and (33), precede nouns just like adjectives but, whereas a determiner points out which entity is meant (it specifies), an adjective describes the quality (it modifies). When both a determiner and an adjective precede a noun, the determiner always precedes the adjective, as in (34a), and not the other way round, as in (34b) (indicated by the asterisk).

(34) a. **Their** irritating owl ate my delicious food.
      b. * Irritating **their** owl ate delicious my food.

Interrogatives such as *whose* in *whose books*, *what* in *what problems*, and *which* in *which computer* are determiners. Quantifiers such as *any, many, much,* and *all* are usually considered determiners, e.g. in *much work, many people,* and *all research.* Some are used before other determiners, namely, *all, both,* and *half,* as in (35). These quantifiers are called pre-determiners, and abbreviated Pre-D. Finally, quantifiers may be adjectival, as in *the many problems* and in (36).

(35) **All** the books; **half** that man's money; **both** those problems.

(36) The challenges are **many/few.**

Numerals are sometimes determiners, as in *two books,* and sometimes more like adjectives, as in *my two books.* Table 2.5 shows the determiners in the order in which they may appear. There are three quantifiers that appear before definite articicles, demonstratives, and possessives and these are labeled pre-determiners. I have added the category adjective to the table since some of the words that are clear determiners can also be adjectives (e.g. appear after copula verbs). The categories are not always completely clear-cut, and (37) sheds some light on the difference.

Table 2.5 Determiners

	Pre-D	D	Post-D or Adj
quantifier	all, both half	some, many, all, few(er) any, much, no, every, less, etc.	many, few
article		the, a	
demonstrative		that, this, those, these	
possessive		my, etc., NP's	
interrogative		whose, what, which, etc.	
numeral		one, two, etc.	one, two, etc.

(37) **The Determiner-Adjective Rule**
      A Determiner points to the noun it goes with or who it belongs to;
      An Adjective gives background information about the noun.

In this book, and in current generative grammar, the category of T stands for Tense and this category contains the finiteness, tense, and agreement information. T can house auxiliaries, when it is finite, and the infinitival marker *to*, when it is non-finite. We'll first look into finiteness and then at the kinds of auxiliaries English has.

The difference between finite and non-finite clauses can be seen as follows. A complete sentence consists of a subject and a finite verb. A finite verb agrees with the subject (which is only visible in the present tense) and indicates present or past. Its subject has nominative case, which can only be seen in the case of pronouns in Modern English, i.e. the subject pronoun of finite verbs must be nominative *I, you, he, she, it, we* and *they*, not accusative *me, him, her, us* or *them* (*you* and *it* are both nominative and accusative). Table 2.6 provides all personal and possessive pronouns in English.

Table 2.6 The case of personal and possessive pronouns

	1S	2S	3S	1P	2P	3P
Nominative (subject)	I	you	he, she, it	we	you	they
Accusative (object)	me	you	him, her, it	us	you	them
Genitive (possessive)	my (mine)	your(s)	his, her(s), its	our(s)	your(s)	their(s)

Finite sentences include a finite verb or a verb group with one finite verb as its first (or only) member. A verb group is centered around a lexical verb, *going* in (38), but it is *have* that makes the entire sentence finite.

(38)   I [**have** been going] there frequently.   finite sentence with finite verb *have*

Have is finite in (38) because it shows subject agreement (*have* rather than *has*, as in (39)), indicates present tense (*have* rather than *had*, as in (40)), and has a nominative subject (*I* rather than *me*, as in the ungrammatical (41)).

(39)   He **has** been going there frequently.

(40)   He **had** been going there frequently.

(41)   *Me have been going there frequently.

Note that in some varieties of English, sentences such as (41) are grammatical.

Modals, as in (42), are finite even though (for historical reasons) they never display subject-verb agreement.

(42)   I **might** have done that.

Only finite sentences are complete sentences. Most of us, however, use fragments in informal speech, in poetry, e.g. Carl Sandburg in the excerpt in (43) from *Follies*, or even in formal writing.

> (43) Shaken,
>   The blossoms of lilac,
>   And shattered,
>   The atoms of purple.
>   Green dip the leaves,
>   Darker the bark,
>   Longer the shadows.

Nevertheless, incomplete sentences are generally frowned upon in formal writing. Sentence (44) below is not a complete sentence but is a sentence fragment.

(44) Mentioning syntactic trees yesterday.

Sentence (55) can become a full sentence by adding a subject and a finite verb as in (45).

(45) **I was** mentioning syntactic trees yesterday.

As will be shown in a later chapter, non-finite sentences can only be part of other sentences. It is always a good idea to count the number of lexical verbs. For instance, how many lexical verbs are there in (46)?

(46) I have heard her sing too often.

In (46), there are two lexical verbs, *heard* and *sing*, and only the first verb group is finite since *have* is finite (e.g. the subject of *have* is nominative *I*). The verb group that *sing* is the sole member of is non-finite since its subject is accusative *her*.

Other sentences that include a non-finite verb are (47) and (48), with the non-finite verbs in bold. Note that the infinitive marker *to* is part of the verb group.

(47) **Seeing** the ordinary as extraordinary is something we all like to do.

(48) She forgot **to google** them.

In (47), *seeing*, *is*, *like*, and *do* are lexical verbs, but only *is* and *like* are finite. In (48), *forgot* and *google* are the lexical verbs, but only *forgot* is finite.

A sentence can contain many verb groups, a (potentially) indefinite number if the speaker had enough energy and could continue, as in (49). This shows the recursive nature of language, as mentioned in Chapter 1.

(49) I noticed that she mentioned that he was saying that she should tell him …

Imperatives are used to order someone to do something. They often lack a subject, as in (50), but this need not be the case, as (51) shows. Imperatives are complete sentences and not sentence fragments.

(50) Draw the trees for these sentences.

(51)   You, draw trees for this.

As its name implies, the auxiliary verb functions to help another verb, but does not itself contribute greatly to the meaning of the sentence. Verbs such as *have, be,* and *do* can be full verbs, as in (52), or auxiliaries, as in (53). In (52), *have* has a meaning 'to possess' and occurs without any other lexical verb. In (53), on the other hand, *have* does not mean 'possess' or 'hold', but contributes to the grammatical meaning of the sentence, namely past tense with present relevance. The same is true for *be* in (54); it contributes to the grammatical meaning emphasizing the continuous nature of the event.

(52)   I **have** a book in my hand.

(53)   I **have** worked here for 15 years.

(54)   That reindeer may **be** working too hard.

Because auxiliaries help other verbs (except when they are main verbs as in (52)), they cannot occur on their own, as the ungrammaticality of (55) shows.

(55)   *I must a book.

The characteristics of auxiliaries in English are summarized in Table 2.7 and a list of some of them appears in Table 2.8.

Table 2.7 Characteristics of auxiliary verbs

a.	They must be used with a lexical verb (unless the verb is elided)
b.	They have little meaning; rather, they express tense, mood, and aspect
c.	They invert in questions, as in *Are you going?*
d.	They occur before *n't*, as in *You aren't going.*
e.	They are used in tags, as in *You are going, aren't you?*
f.	They are used for emphasis, as in *If you do go, let me know.*

Table 2.8 Auxiliaries in English

modal:	may, might, can could, shall, should, will, would, must
semi-modal:	have to, ought to, wanna, gonna, need, dare, etc. (these do not invert)
perfect:	have
progressive:	be
dummy:	do
passive:	be, get

Coordinators are relatively simple and join similar categories or phrases. Complementizers introduce subordinate clauses and look remarkably similar to prepositions and adverbs. We abbreviate both as C.

Coordinators such as *and* and *or* join two elements of the same kind, e.g. the nouns in (56).

(56) Rigobertha **and** Pablo went to Madrid **or** Barcelona.

They are also sometimes called coordinating conjunctions, as in Figure 2.2, but in this book, we'll use coordinator. There are also two-part coordinators such as *both … and, either … or*, and *neither … nor*.

FOXTROT

Figure 2.2. Connecting sentences

Complementizers such as *that, because, whether, if*, and *since* join two clauses where one clause is subordinate to the other, as in (57). The subordinate clause is indicated by means of brackets.

(57) Rigobertha and Pablo left [**because** Isabella was about to arrive].

They are also called subordinating conjunctions or subordinators. We will use complementizer. Like prepositions, coordinators and complementizers are invariable in English (i.e. never have an ending), but complementizers introduce a new clause whereas prepositions are connected to a noun. Some examples of complementizers and some of their other functions (if they have them) are provided in Table 2.9.

Table 2.9 A few complementizers

C	example of C use	other use	example of other use
after	**After** she left, it rained.	preposition	**after** him
as	Fair **as** the moon is, it …	degree adverb	**as** nice
because	(43)	–	
before	**Before** it snowed, it rained.	preposition	**before** me
for	I expect **for** you to do that.	preposition	**for** Santa
if	**If** she wins, that will be great	–	
so	He was tired, **so** he went to sleep	adverb	**so** tired
that	I know **that** the earth is round.	determiner	**that** book
when	I wonder **when** it will happen.	adverb	He left **when**?
while	She played soccer, **while** he slept	noun	A short **while**

We can now formulate another rule, namely the one in (58).

(58) **The Preposition-Complementizer-Adverb Rule**
A Preposition introduces a noun (e.g. **about** *the book*);
a Complementizer introduces a sentence (e.g. **because** *he left*); and
an Adverb is on its own (e.g. *She went* **out**; and **Unfortunately**, *she left*).

These categories are often ambiguous in Modern English because prepositions and adverbs can change to complementizers.

3. Pronouns

Pronouns are a hybrid category since they do not carry much lexical meaning but they can function on their own, unlike articles, auxiliaries, and complementizers, which need something to follow them. This makes them hard to classify as lexical or grammatical categories.

Personal pronouns, such as *I, me, she, he* and *it*, and reflexive pronouns, such as *myself, yourself,* and *herself,* are seen as grammatical categories by many (myself included). The reason is that they don't mean very much: they are used to refer to phrases already mentioned. However, personal and reflexive pronouns are similar to nouns, since they function as Subjects and Objects. Thus, a determiner such as *the* cannot stand on its own, but *she*, as in (59), can.

(59) **She** knows that **she's** a con artist   (COCA 2012 ABC)

Personal pronouns can be divided according to number into singular and plural and according to person into first, second, and third person. For example, *I* and *me* are first person singular, and *we* and *us* are first person plural. The second person pronoun *you* is used both as singular and as plural. Third person singular pronouns *he/him*, *she/her*, and *it* are further divided according to gender; the third person plural pronouns *they* and *them* do not distinguish gender. Refer to Table 2.6 for a summary of the different personal pronouns.

Some pronouns look like the determiners we saw in the previous section. Almost all determiners, except the articles, can stand on their own, e.g. demonstratives, such as *that* in *that is a problem*. Thus, they are very much like pronouns but they can also have a noun following.

Apart from personal and reflexive pronouns, there are some possessive pronouns that occur on their own, and are therefore not determiners. Examples are *mine, yours, his, hers, ours*, and *theirs*, as in (60a). These pronouns appear when the noun they specify has been left unspecified. Thus, (60a) could be rewritten as (60b), with *mine* replaced by *my mess*.

(60)   a.   That mess is not **mine**, but it is **yours**.
        b.   That mess is not my mess, but it is your mess.

The result is awkward, however, and I will suggest that *mine* and *yours* are really independent pronouns, not determiners with the noun left out.

The other determiners, namely interrogatives, quantifiers, and numerals can occur independently too, as in (61). It will be up to you as the reader to decide whether these are independent pronouns or are really determiners preceding nouns that have been left out.

(61)   **What** would be solved if **all** chose **two**?

Indefinite pronouns, such as *anyone, anybody, everyone, someone, something*, and *nothing*, occur frequently and are in many ways similar to personal pronouns. There are many other indefinites that are similar to adverbs, e.g. *anywhere, nowhere, sometime*, and *somewhere*, or to degree adverbs, e.g. *somewhat*. They are *pro*-forms and can stand in for an adverb.

As for the labels, this book will label something a determiner if it can have a noun following it but a pronoun if it can't. In a tree, it'll use D for determiner and DP for pronoun (though some people use D for both).

4.   Conclusion

This chapter reviews how to distinguish the basic building blocks of English that we'll use to build phrases in the next chapter. We've seen a lot of ambiguity among lexical categories. For instance, nouns can often be verbs because English has lost many of the endings that earlier made nouns and verbs distinguishable.

Rules such as (58), repeated here as (62), are needed because grammatical categories and semi-grammatical categories such as prepositions are also often ambiguous. I have added the description for determiner from (37).

(62) **The P/C/A/D Rule**
A Preposition introduces a noun;
a Complementizer introduces a sentence; an Adverb is on its own; and
a Determiner points to the noun it goes with and who it belongs to.

Let's look at the ambiguity of *that*. It can be a complementizer (*I know **that** he left*) and a determiner (***that** book*). The word *for* can be a complementizer (*I expected **for** him to do that*) and a preposition (***for** that reason*). Many other examples exist, e.g. the complementizer *before* can be a preposition, an adverb, and a noun (according to the *Oxford English Dictionary*).

At the end of this chapter you should be able to label the categories of the words in any English text and provide reasons for your answers.

Exercises

A.   Look at the below text and identify the lexical verbs and prepositions.

> Text
> Mayor Mark Mitchell and the Tempe City Council recently approved a 20-year agreement with SolarCity that will put Tempe on the map as an energy efficient city. Mitchell and the council hope the approval will advance the city's plan to provide 20 percent of energy through renewable sources by 2025. "We just recently installed solar panels on the fire and courts building and we are just now breaking ground on the Library Complex Solar Project, which will provide about 35 percent of energy to the complex," said Tempe Public Information Officer Melissa Quillard.
>
> (from the East Valley Tribune, 5 November 2015)

B.   Do the same for the C-elements and adverbs.

C.   In sentence (22) of Section 1, which interpretation has your preference?

D.   Which verbs in the text of A are finite?

More challenging

E.   Select a text in a language other than English (100 words) and provide word-by-word glosses. Then identify the determiners and prepositions (or postpositions).

Chapter 3

Structure and hierarchy

Keywords: Phrases headed by lexical and grammatical categories (NP, VP, AP, PP and DP, TP, CP), X-bar theory, structural hierarchy, c-command, negative polarity, reflexive, grammatical functions of phrases (subject, object, predicate, adverbial)

Sentences can be divided into groups of words that belong together. The group of words is called a phrase. If the most important part of the phrase, i.e. the head, is an adjective, the phrase is an Adjective Phrase; if the most important part of the phrase is a noun, the phrase is a Noun Phrase, and so on. A structural representation of a sentence expresses which words go together and what modifies what; it renders the sentence clearer and less ambiguous. One could indicate structures by putting brackets around phrases, but that gets confusing when the sentence is complex. Instead, we use 'trees' because they are more transparent.

The main goal of this chapter is to explain how the words we have seen in Chapter 2 can combine into phrases and build trees. A second aim is to look at how structural hierarchies are responsible for certain linguistic phenomena. A final goal is to distinguish the different functions that a phrase can have, which can be discovered by looking at the tree.

The outline is as follows. In Section 1, we look at basic phrases, first for those where the head is a lexical category and then for those where the head is a functional category. The section ends with testing phrases and a way of looking at the structure of phrases that is known as X-bar Theory. Having seen how to construct a tree for a basic sentence in Section 1, we turn to movement of phrases in Section 2. The hierarchy of trees can explain a number of phenomena, e.g. which nouns can serve as antecedents and when negative polarity items can be used. This is discussed in Section 3. Section 4 discusses a point from traditional grammar, namely that phrases have grammatical functions in the sentence. Section 5 is a conclusion.

1.   Phrases

In this section, I show that the categories from Chapter 2 can be used to build phrases and sentences. After considering the lexical categories in 1.1 and the grammatical ones in 1.2, we test structure and constituents in 1.3, and we look at a way to account for the uniformity of the phrases through what is known as X′ theory (pronounced as X-bar). The latter system was until recently seen as part of Universal Grammar but, with the recent change towards having less in Universal Grammar, this is no longer the case. We will also discuss the move towards bare structures.

1.1   The Phrase (for lexical categories)

A Noun Phrase (NP) such as *the nice unicorn* is built around a noun, namely, *unicorn*. This noun (N) is called the head of the NP. We can find the head in a simple way by thinking how we'd shorten the phrase and still keep the essential part, as in a telegram. For instance, we might shorten (1) to (2).

(1)   [The nice unicorns from that planet] are visiting us regularly.

(2)   Unicorns visit regularly.

In addition to the head, NPs can contain determiners (e.g. *the*) and adjectives (*nice*). A tree structure for a simple NP is given in (3). The lines, called 'branches', indicate how the phrase is divided up, and branches come together in 'nodes'.

(3)

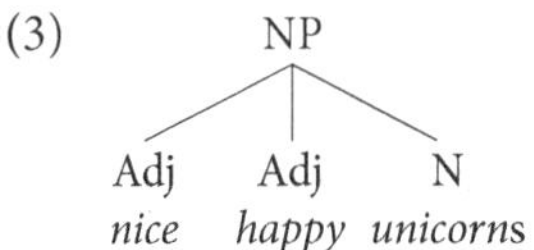

A structure such as (4) expresses the relationships more accurately than (3), however. In (3), it is unclear whether *nice* is more closely connected to the adjective *happy* or the noun *unicorns*, but from (4), it is clear that *nice* specifies *happy unicorns*. A structure as in (3) with more than two branches is a flat structure since the hierarchies are not clear.

(4)

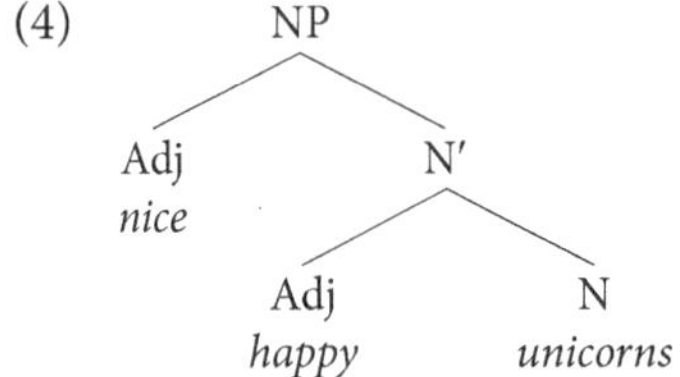

There are a number of things to note. First, the top node of (4), i.e. where the branches come together, is an NP because the head of the phrase is an N. Shortening the NP, as in a headline, would tell us that. Secondly, the node in between the NP and N is called N′ (pronounced N-bar). It is an intermediate node. Third, note that *nice* and *happy* in (4) are themselves heads of Adjective Phrases and we could indicate that as in (5).

(5)
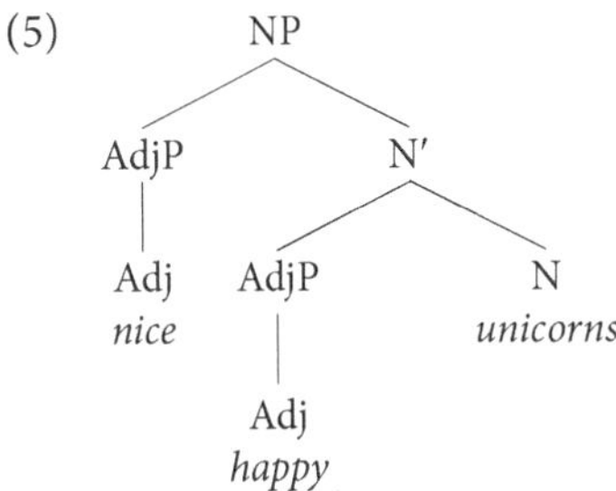

One way to go about constructing this tree is (a) to find the head *unicorns*, (b) to label the entire phrase as NP, and (c) to draw branches from the NP down to AdjP on the left and, if there is more than one word left, to N′ on the right. The N′ functions as placeholder until the N can be put down.

On occasion, it may be hard to find the head of an NP, or to identify the entire NP. For instance, the initial group of words in (6), adapted from one of Dr. Seuss' books, is centered around the noun *wocket*.

(6)   [The pleasant wocket in my pocket that I adore] loves cranberry chutney.

Wocket is the head because if you had to shorten the sentence, you might say *the wocket loves chutney*. Thus, *pleasant* and *in my pocket* and *that I adore* add additional information. Another way to shorten the sentence is to use a pronoun, as in (7). This is called pronominalization. If the group of words in *the pleasant wocket in my pocket that I adore* can be replaced by one pronoun, it has to be a phrase.

(7)   It loves cranberry chutney.

You can also find the entire phrase by examining which parts say something about the head, i.e. modify it. For instance, in (6), both *pleasant* and *in my pocket* have no other function in the sentence than to modify the head *wocket*.

An important function of the head of the NP is to determine the agreement with the verb. I have adapted (1) as (8) with brackets indicating that the head of the subject NP is *unicorns*. The singular and plural number underneath the nouns and verb show that the head of the NP, *unicorns,* agrees with the auxiliary verb *are* in (plural) number, not the closer noun *planet*:

(8)   [The nice [unicorns] from that planet]   are visiting us regularly.
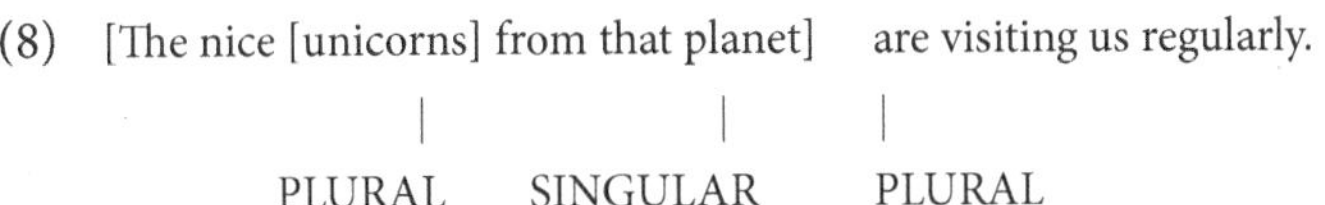

We could represent (6) as (9), where I have left the *that I adore* out for simplicity.

(9)

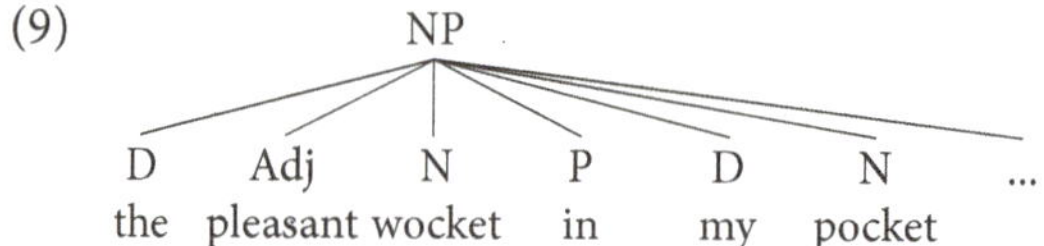

This structure indicates that the phrase is composed of six words, but it does not say whether *in* is more connected to *my pocket* or to *wocket*. This is again a flat structure since we don't see what goes with what. It is even worse than (3). Therefore, we will avoid this kind of tree. Figure 3.1 shows why we need to keep track of what modifies what. The adjective *vegetarian* can go with *chicken* or with *soup!*

Figure 3.1 Vegetarian Chickens <http://blondie.com/comics/november-5-2002>
Blondie: © 2002 King Features Syndicate, Inc.

As we'll see in Section 1.2, the D is the real head of the phrase that includes the NP, which I have shown in (10a–b). These trees provide clear, hierarchical structures for the sentence. The N′ levels are (again) needed because the NP contains more than two parts.

(10) a.

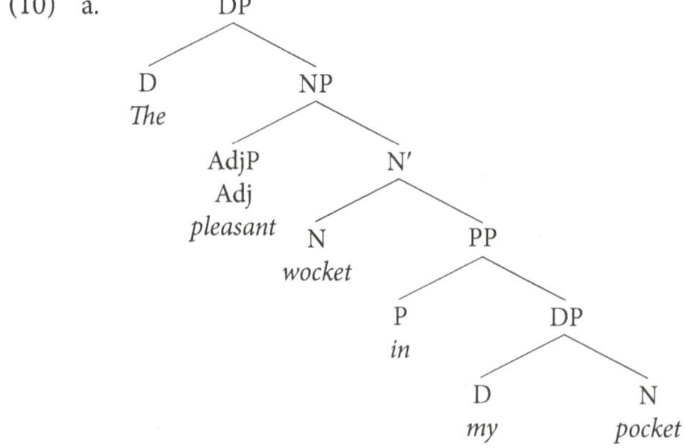

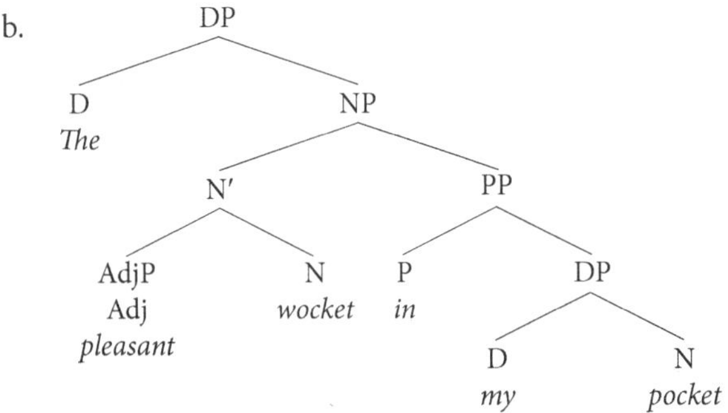

In (10a), *in my pocket* goes together with *wocket*. In a structure, this close connection is expressed by having the line, i.e. 'branch', that goes upwards connect to the same point, i.e. 'node'. This means they are 'sisters' in the structure. In (10b), *pleasant* and *wocket* are put closer together, i.e. are sisters. Both structures are possible but we'll come back to this in Chapter 7 to argue that (10a) is a better representation. The meaning difference between (10a) and (10b) is minimal, but this is not always the case as sentences such as (20) below show. Note again that *pleasant* is itself the head of a phrase, which I indicate by means of and Adj head inside an AdjP. The ultimate tree is not as important as understanding why you represent a tree in a particular way, as I have just tried to do for (10). (At the end of the chapter, in (59), we modify (10a–b) to have the PP and AdjP be sisters to N′, not to N).

Pronouns and names such as *Jennifer*, *Edward*, and *Malacandra* cannot have other elements modify/specify them and therefore we will see them as full phrases, as in (11a–b). They are not lexical because they refer to nouns but do not have semantic features themselves. That's why they are DPs and not NPs.

(11) a.   DP
           |
           she

     b.   DP
           |
           Malacandra

Under very special circumstances, proper names can be modified, as when there are many persons called *Edward* and you want to make sure it is *the nice Edward*. This is not common with names, and it is very uncommon with pronouns in English.

Some heads are trickier to identify than others. For instance, in *one of those pages*, the head is *one*, and in *a piece of paper*, *piece* is the head. Frequently, a relative clause, such as *who wore that ugly hat* in (12) is part of another phrase, as shown by brackets, modifying the head *person*.

(12)   [The person [who wore that ugly hat]] is the queen.

AdjPs are built around adjectives, which indicate properties of nouns; AdvPs are built around adverbs which indicate qualities of verbs, adverbs, and adjectives. Since adjectives and adverbs have this qualifying function, they themselves are (optionally) accompanied by a degree marker such as *very, too, extremely, really*. The latter are adverbs of a special kind: they always modify another adverb or adjective and never modify a verb. They are comparable to the determiner in the NP, and more like grammatical than lexical categories. They do not expand into an AdvP of their own since degree markers such as *extremely very* do not occur.

An example of an AdjP is given in (13a) and of an AdvP in (13b). The (D)Adv indicates a degree adverb but, from now on, just Adv will be used.

(13)   a.

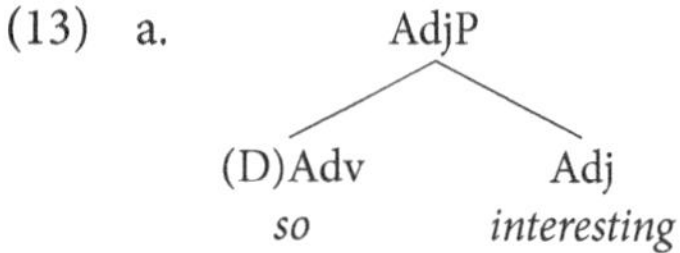

       b.

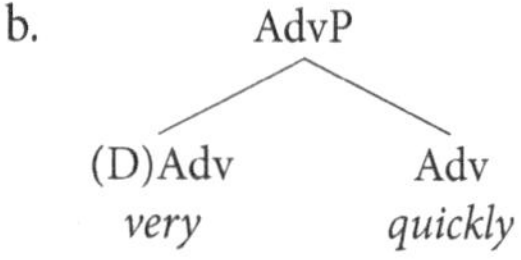

In (13a), the head of the AdjP is the adjective *interesting*, and this head is modified by a degree adverb *so*; in (13b), the adverb *quickly* expands into a phrase and is modified by the degree adverb *very* that, like *so* in (13a), does not form a phrase of its own. That's why I choose not to make *so* and *very* the heads of an AdvP.

An AdjP and AdvP can be pronominalized, as in (14) and (15) respectively, using *so*.

(14)   I was happy and **so** was she.

(15)   He behaved nicely, and **so** did she.

Turning to VPs, they are built around a verb, which can indicate an action, as in (16a), a state, as in (16b), or a sensation, as in (16c). Verbs can be in the present or past tense (they are past in (16a–b–c)). Some VPs include other obligatory material, i.e. words or phrases that cannot easily be left out, such as the DP in (16a), the PP in (16b), and the AdjP in (16c). These obligatory parts are called complements.

(16) a.

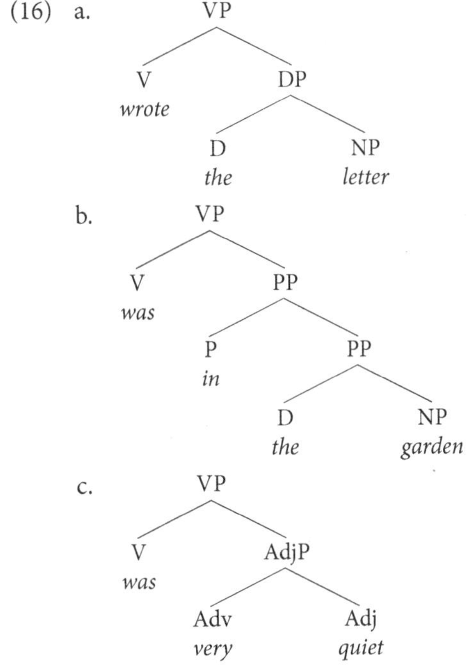

The VP can also include optional material that explains when, where, why, and how the action or state that the verb describes took place. These optional elements function as adverbials.

As in the case of the DP, AdjP, and AdvP, a VP can be pronominalized. An example is given in (17), where the (bolded) VP *washed the dishes* is replaced by *do so*. Some linguists call these pro-VPs or pro-forms, since they do not stand for nouns. It is up to you whether you call them pronoun or pro-form.

(17)   Gijsbert **washed the dishes** and Marieken **did so** as well.

A PP is built around a preposition. As mentioned in the previous section, prepositions indicate relations in space and time. PPs include a P, an NP, and a DP, as in (18).

(18)

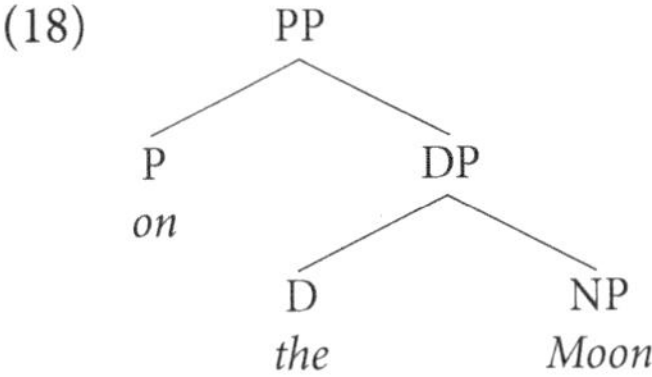

PPs can be replaced (pronominalized) by the adverbs such as *then, when, how,* and *there.*

Up to now, we have looked at the names of categories and phrases, e.g. N and NP. Depending on where phrases are situated in the tree, they play a particular function, such as subject and object. Functions will not be put in the tree structure because it should be clear from the tree what they are. We'll delve into identifying functions in Section 4 but, since the structure of PPs depends on their function, we need to go into a little of that here as well.

With respect to PPs, it is not always easy to determine what role they play and their function in a sentence is manifold. For instance, in the ambiguous (19), an often used sentence in linguistic circles, does the PP function inside the NP, or are the NP and PP independent of one another?

(19)   She saw the hobbit with glasses.

The answer to both questions can be 'yes' because the sentence is ambiguous. In the one case, the PP *with glasses* modifies the *hobbit* and functions inside the DP *the hobbit with glasses*; in the other case, the PP is independent of the N since it modifies the VP and specifies how the seeing was done. The structure for the former reading is as in (20a) and for the latter reading as in (20b).

(20)   a.

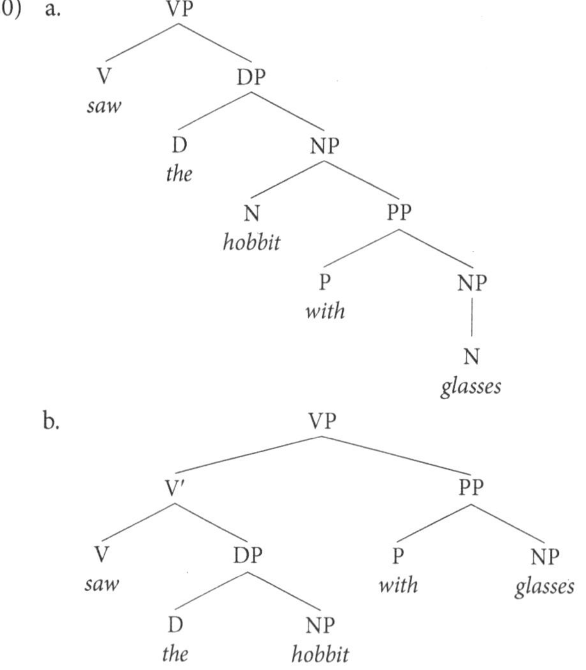

   b.

Thus, a particular tree structure disambiguates the sentence. In (20a), the PP *with glasses* is right next to the N *hobbit* (i.e. the PP is sister to N) and therefore modifies *hobbit*; in (20b), the same PP is right next to the V′ *saw the hobbit* (i.e. the PP is sister to V′) and hence says something on how the seeing of the man is done. For now, don't worry about (20b) too much. You may have noticed the use of V′ (pronounced V-bar) in (20b). A V′ (like the N′ in an NP) is an intermediate category in the VP. In (20b), we need to group the V and NP together so we need a label for that and we use a 'small VP' or placeholder until we can put down a branch for the V.

1.2   Phrases of functional/grammatical categories

In the previous section, it has been shown how lexical categories, such as N, project to a phrase. In the late 1980s, grammatical categories, such as D(eterminer), C(omplementizer), and T(ense) also came to be seen as the heads of phrases. So, a C such as *that* is the head of the CP, a D such as *the* is the head of the DP, which we have already seen in the previous section, and an AUX such as *have* is the head of the TP. As in the case of lexical categories, there are intermediate categories, such as C′, D′, and T′.

The T forms the core of the basic sentence, which looks like (21) where I have also added DPs. The T includes information on whether the sentence is finite or past or present. These features are shown in (21b) but are not always explicitly marked in every tree we derive.

(21)   a.

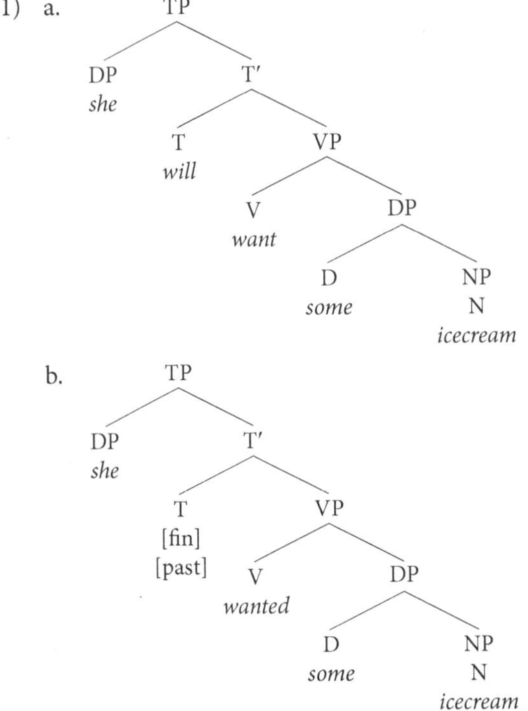

The C and CP are needed to ask questions, as we'll see later, and also to include embedded sentences, as in (22).

(22)

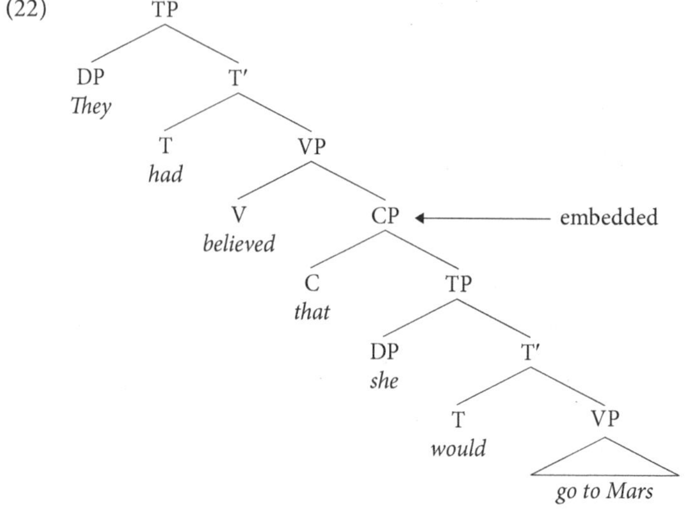

Other trees where one clause is part of another clause are shown in (23) and (24).

(23)

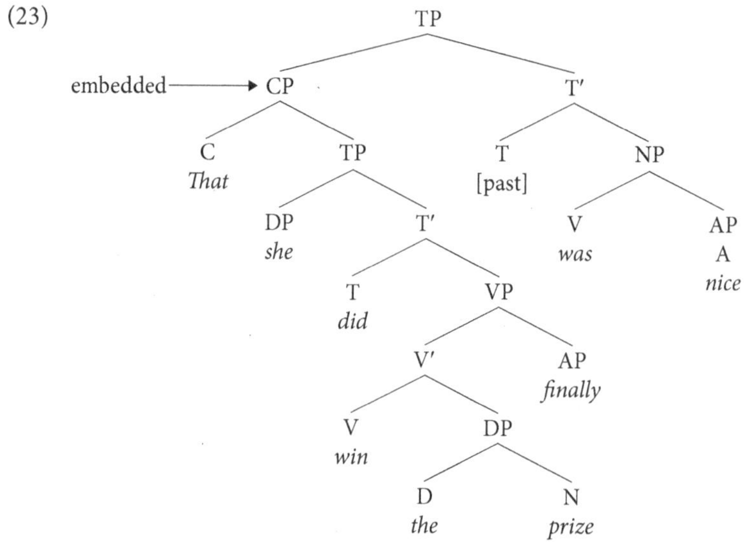

(24)

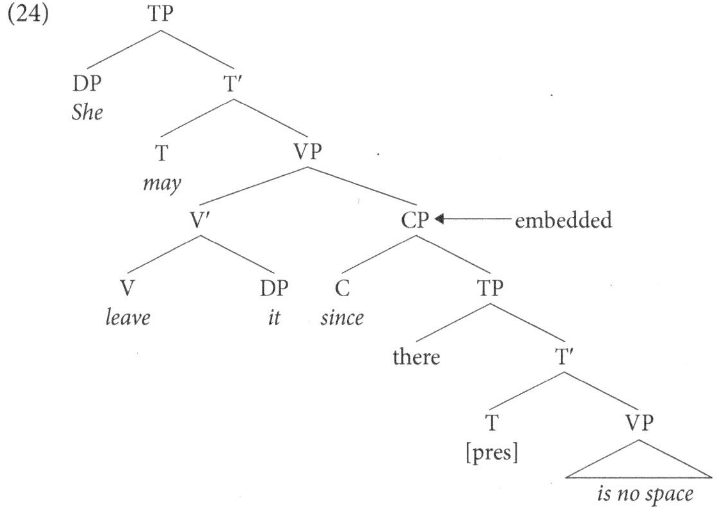

To conclude, T is the head of the TP and shows if a sentence is finite or not, and its tense; C links the TP to another sentence or indicates that the sentence is a question, as we'll see later in this chapter and in Chapter 6.

1.3   Testing and X′

A phrase is a group of words forming a unit and is united around a head, e.g. a noun or a verb. Since phrases are syntactic units, a number of rules apply to them. We discuss that now after which we'll look at some similarities between phrases.

Five rules are listed in Table 3.1. I'll apply them to some of the phrases in (25).

(25)   She ran to the store.

For instance, if I have a hunch that *to the store* is a phrase, I can test that by pronominalizing *to the store* as *there*, coordinate it, delete it, replace it, and move it, as shown in the table. The same is true for the VP.

Table 3.1 Finding a phrase

		PP	VP
a.	it can be pronominalized:	*She ran [there]*	*She [did so]*
b.	it can be coordinated with a phrase of the same kind:	*She ran [to the bookstore] and [to the library]*;	*She [ran to the store] and [yelled]*
c.	it can be deleted:	*She ran [...]*;	She wants to [...]
d.	Replaceable by a *wh*-element:	*[Where] did she run?*	not applicable
e.	it can be moved:	*[To the store] she ran.*	[Run to the store] she did

The five criteria in Table 3.1 confirm that *to the store* in (25) is a phrase and four confirm that the VP is. All phrases can be pronominalized and coordinated, as shown in Table 3.2.

Table 3.2 Pronominalization and coordination of phrases

	pronominalization by:	coordination:
DP/NP	s/he, it, who, what	the cat and the dog
VP	do so	wrote a book and read the paper
PP	there, then, where, when	to Mary and to John
AP	how, so	quickly and happily (adjective); soon and often (adverb)
CP	it	I know that he left and that she arrived

However, not all phrases can be deleted or replaced by a *wh*-element. The initial DP is very important, and in English, sentences are ungrammatical without it. Thus, changing (25) into (26) produces an ungrammatical sentence (unless it is a topic, as in diaries).

(26) What happened?
 *Ran to the store.

The reason is that English is not a pro-drop language, as we also saw in Chapter 1, and is not connected to *she* being a phrase or not.

Phrases have heads, both lexical and grammatical heads. Most heads have complements, e.g. a verb has an object in (20) and (21) above. The same is true with T and C. C has TP as complement and T has VP. If we consider the TP, we notice another position, namely the one that the subject is in. This position is called the specifier position and it is present with all phrases. With the Specifier added, the structure of a phrase is a head, a complement, a specifier, and optionally an adverbial (also called adjunct or modifier), as in (27).

(27)

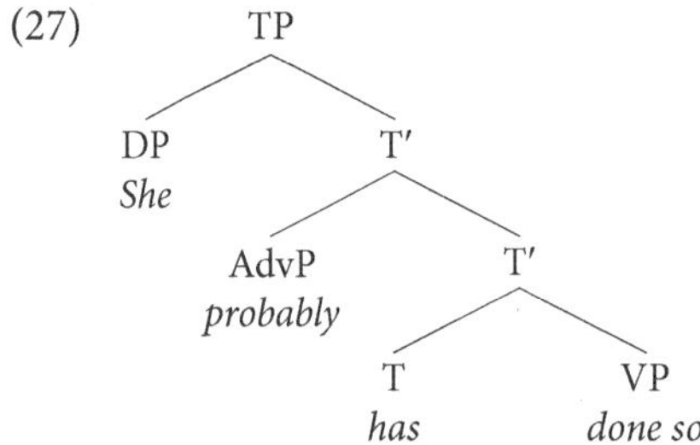

The fact that structures look very similar is sometimes explained by resorting to X′ structure, and generalized as (28), where X can be replaced by N, V, C, T, etc.

(28)

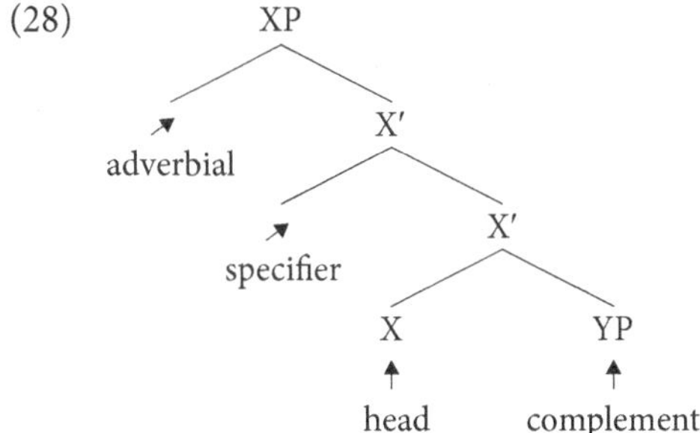

In (28), the adverbial is a sister of X′. An alternative is to adjoin it above the XP, as in (29a). This process is called Chomsky-adjunction. Actual words have been added to the structure in (29b).

(29) a.

b.

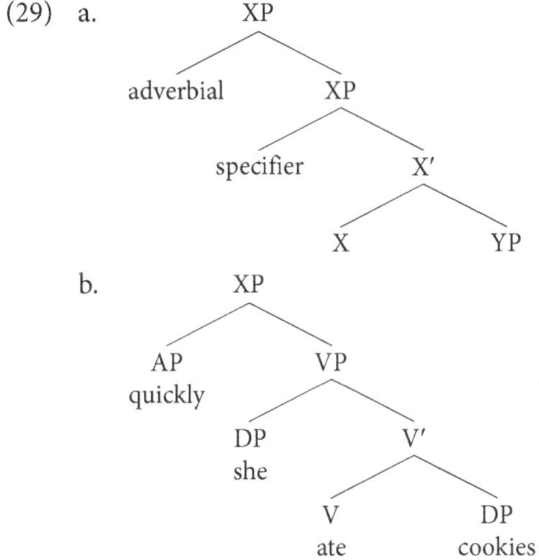

In this section, we have so far identified groups of words that go together as phrases. Each of the categories we have seen in Chapter 2 can project to a phrase and their internal organization is fairly uniform, as shown in (28).

X-bar structures provide much insight into the uniformity of the different categories and account for differences between languages in an elegant way. For instance, some languages can be described as head-initial (VO) and others head-final (OV). The Minimalist Program, as mentioned in Chapter 1, tries to attribute as little as possible to Universal Grammar and emphasizes the free merging of categories where tree starts bottom-to-top. This results in a departure from (28) and in what is called 'Bare Phrase Structure'. Bare Phrase Structure takes words from the lexicon and merges them without the projection and labelling of (28). This is something to keep in mind when reading research couched in the most recent model, but for our purposes of making the structure clear, we will follow X-bar structure because it clarifies the structure and the labels.

2.   Movement

With the trees in Section 1, we can build a basic sentence structure (e.g. *I eat apples*). However, to ask a question or to front something to give it prominence, the basic structure has to be rearranged through movement. Movement is highly constrained: heads move to other head positions, as we'll see in 2.1, phrases move to other phrase positions, as we'll see in 2.2, and movement can't be too far.

2.1   Yes/No questions

In *yes/no* questions, the only appropriate answer is *Yes* or *No* (or *perhaps/maybe*). To make such a question, e.g. of (30a), the auxiliary is fronted, as in (30b), through head-movement of T to C.

> (30)   a.   She has gone.
> b.   **Has** she gone?

If there is no auxiliary present, as in (31a), a dummy *do* is used, as in (31b).

> (31)   a.   You saw Santa.
> b.   **Did** you see Santa?

A structure for *yes/no* questions is given in (32), where the auxiliary moves to C (indicated by the struck-through copy that is left in T). The C has Q(uestion)-features which the auxiliary-movement makes clear.

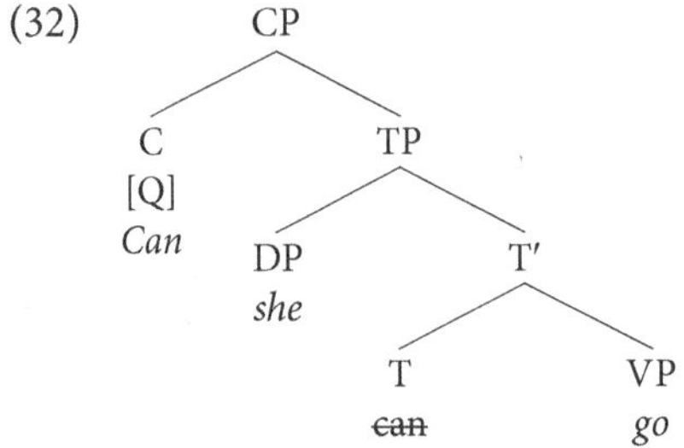

One piece of evidence for this movement to C is that when the complementizer is filled, as in subordinate clauses such as (33), this movement is not possible.

> (33)   *I know that can she ~~can~~ go.

As a note to (32), it should be added that, ever since 1995, Chomsky has seen head-movement as problematic because it violates the Extension Condition. The latter says that movement builds on top of the spine that is already created. Chomsky argues that T adjoins to C, as in (34), rather than moving into the position, as in (32). This makes the movement not to the spine of the tree but to a daughter of the spine.

(34)

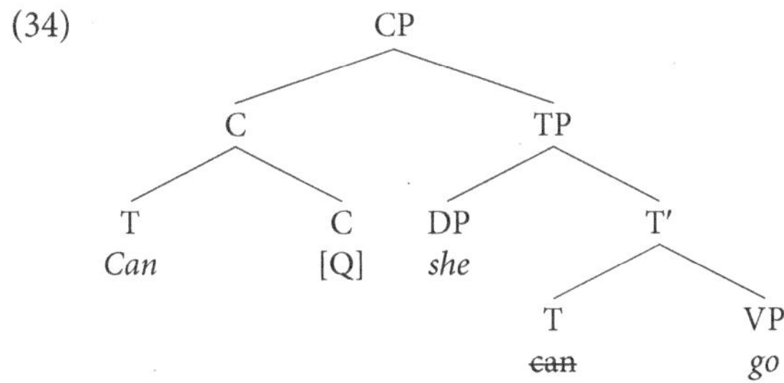

It is not immediately obvious what the solution is and, therefore, we'll continue to use head-movement, as in (32).

2.2   Wh-questions

To ask a content-question, one starts out with a *wh*-word (*who, what, why, when, where, how*), in the specifier of the CP, and an auxiliary in second position, in the head C. There is also a copy left in the original position (struck through). Examples are given in (35) and (36).

(35)   Who will you see ~~who~~?

(36)   How much wood would a wood chuck chuck ~~how much wood~~, if a wood chuck could chuck wood?

A structure for (35) is given in (37), where the *wh*-phrase moves to the specifier of the CP and the auxiliary *will* moves from T to C.

(37)

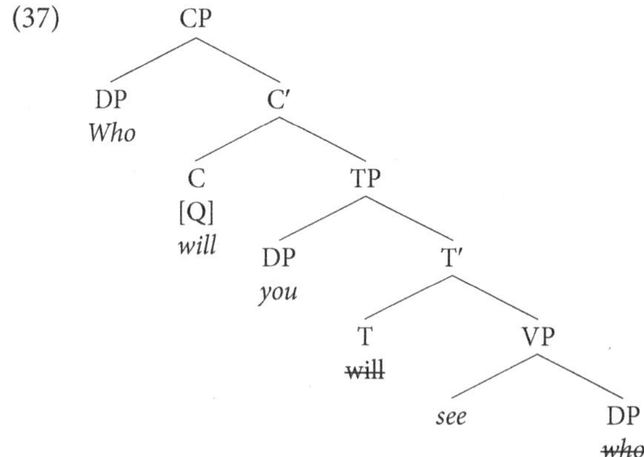

Evidence for the copy is that, with special intonation, movement is not necessary. Thus, (38) is possible with special emphasis on *what*.

(38)   You saw WHAT?

Questions such as (38) are called 'echo-questions'.

Section 2 has examined sentences in which movement takes place, of T to C in (32) and of a *wh*-element to Spec CP in (37).

3.   Hierarchical structural and c-command

In this section, I first provide some evidence that syntax is hierarchically ordered and then provide a definition of structural hierarchy that is necessary in a number of cases. The evidence that the hierarchical, structural representations that we have suggested in the first sections are the right ones comes from question-formation, reflexives, and negative polarity items. These hierarchical structures emerge automatically from the way we merge items, a mechanism provided by Universal Grammar.

To form a *yes/no* question in English, as we have just seen in (32), we need to take an auxiliary and move it to C. So, we start with a declarative sentence, as in (39a) and then move *can*, as in (39b). This auxiliary can't be just any auxiliary, as (39c) shows.

(39)   a.   Eagles that have flown so far can still swim.
       b.   Can eagles that have flown so far __ still swim?
       c.   *Have eagles that __ flown so far can still swim?

(39a), a sentence slightly adapted from one used by Chomsky, consists of two clauses but only the auxiliary that goes with the main clause can be moved to C. This is shown in (39b), with a tree as in (40). The auxiliary that is part of the subordinate relative clause *that have flown so far* cannot move and, if it does, results in the ungrammatical (39c).

(40)

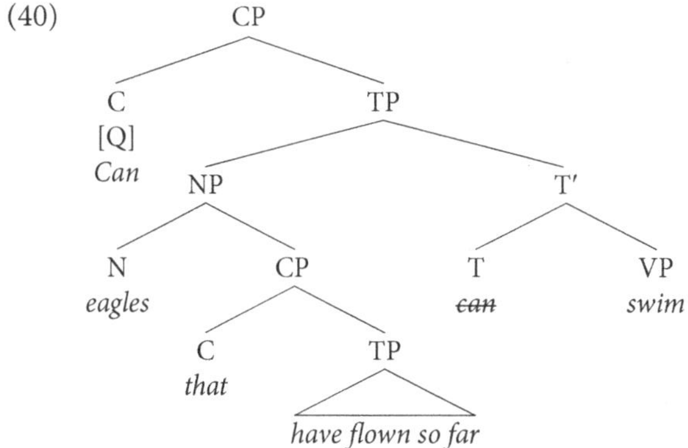

Reflexives refer to antecedents and, in determining the antecedent, hierarchical structure is relevant as well. As was shown in Chapter 1, repeated here as (41), reflexives do not select the closest noun antecedent: *himself* in (41) refers to *husband* not *Jane*. Another example like that appears in (42) where *himself* has an antecedent (*John*) that is quite far away.

(41)   The husband of Jane voted for **himself**.

(42)   John seemed to Mary to have perjured **himself**.

If we draw a tree for (41), the higher DP (in bold) is the phrase that serves as antecedent. The precise definition of what can count as antecedent will be given below.

(43)

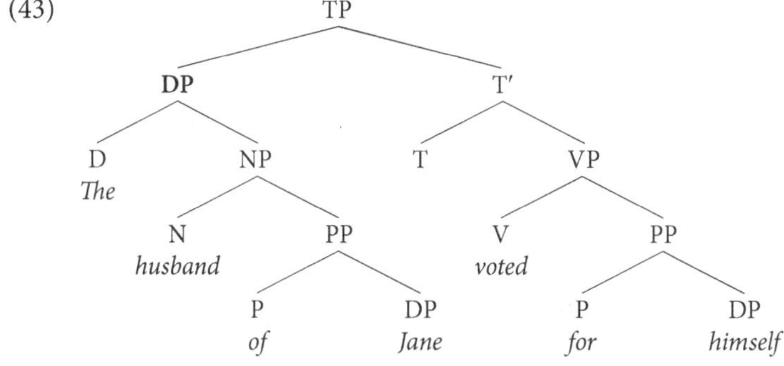

Negative polarity items (NPIs) are words or phrases that need a negative or question environment. The NPIs *ever* in (44) and *any* in (45) exemplify that: the negative or question licenses *ever* and *any* in the (a)-examples. If there is none present, the result is the ungrammatical (b)-examples.

(44)   a.   I won't **ever** do that.
       b.   * I will **ever** do that.

(45)   a.   Does he have **any** idea?
       b.   * He has **any** idea.

To license the NPI, the negative or question word has to be higher in the structure; it can't just precede, as the ungrammaticality of (46) shows, with the tree as in (47a). (47b) gives the tree for the grammatical (44a).

(46) * The people who **can't** find a job will **ever** get benefits.

(47)   a.

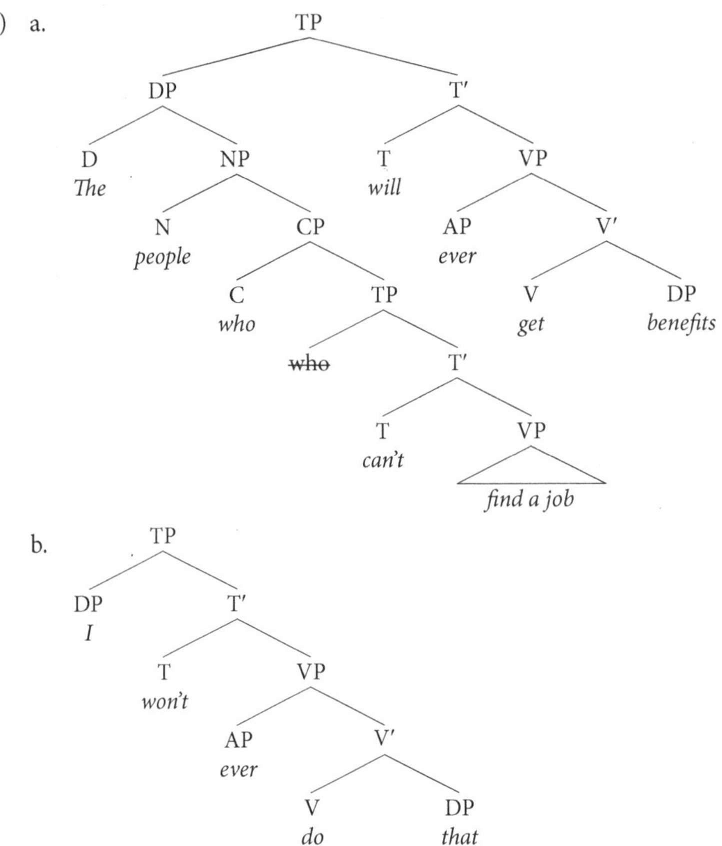

In order to account for the precise relationships of the antecedent in (43) and the negative in (47), we need a definition of c-command, as in (48), adapted from Reinhart (1976).

(48)   A node *a* c-commands a node *b* if every branching node dominating *a* also dominates *b*, and neither *a* nor *b* dominates the other.

In (43), the DP *Jane* is not c-commanding *himself* but the DP *the husband of Jane* is and that determines the reference of the reflexive. The bolded DP (node *a* in (48)) has a TP dominating it and this TP also dominates the reflexive. In (47a), the node dominating the negative is the lower TP which doesn't dominate *ever* but, in (47b), *ever* is c-commanded by the negative because the T′ that dominates *won't* also dominates *ever*.

In short, language is organized using hierarchical structures, as shown in three different constructions. The formation of a question uses the highest auxiliary. The notion of c-command is relevant for reflexives and NPIs because they need to be c-commanded by the antecedent and negative, respectively.

4.   Grammatical functions

This section will discuss the grammatical functions of the phrases. There are four main grammatical functions that can be assigned to constituents or phrases: subjects, objects or complements, predicates, and adverbials or modifiers.

Subjects typically come before the verb since English is an SVO language. They can be distinguished by means of three tests, as shown in Table 3.3, of which we have already seen (b) and (c).

Table 3.3 Subject tests (subject is in italics; verb is in bold)

a. Inversion with the AUX in Yes/No questions *The pig from Malacandra* **will** want to eat soon **Will** *the pig from Malacandra* want to eat soon?
b. Agreement with the Verb/AUX *The pfiftrigg* **is** nice *The pfiftriggs* **are** nice.
c. Nominative case on the subject (only visible on pronouns) *S/he is leaving*

Object/complement is a cover term for a number of functions: direct object, as in (49), indirect object, as in (50), or prepositional object, as in (51). They follow the verb in English.

(49)   I saw [the man with the red hat] in the garden.   Direct object

(50)   I gave [the man with the green hat] some flowers.   Indirect (and direct) object

(51)   I referred [to that article].   Prepostional object

Objects can be passivized, as in (52), and indirect objects can (often) have *to* or *for* precede them, as in (53).

(52)   a.   **The man** was seen (by me) in the garden.   Direct object
     b.   **The man** was given some flowers (by me).   Indirect object
     c.   **The article** was referred to (by me).   Prepositional object

(53)   I gave some flowers **to the man**.

Predicates say something about subjects and are realized by VPs. In (53), *gave some flowers to the man* is such a predicate. When a copula or linking verb is present, the APs, PPs, and DPs that follow it are called subject or object predicates, depending on what they modify. A subject predicate appears in (54) and an object predicate in (55).

(54)   I am [a student with a lot of work].

(55)   I found the students [hard-working].

Adverbials are optional and provide information about when, where, how and why the action took place. Examples can be found in (56).

(56)   He talked to his pet rock [happily][for an hour][while driving home][because he hadn't seen it all day].

They also occur inside phrases and are then typically referred to as modifiers, bracketed in (57). Objects inside phrases are usually called complements.

(57)   The [energetic], [motivated] penguins [from Antarctica].

Functions can be read off the tree, e.g. the sister of the V is its object. The adverbial is the sister of a bar-level category: the PP is sister to a V′ in (58).

(58)

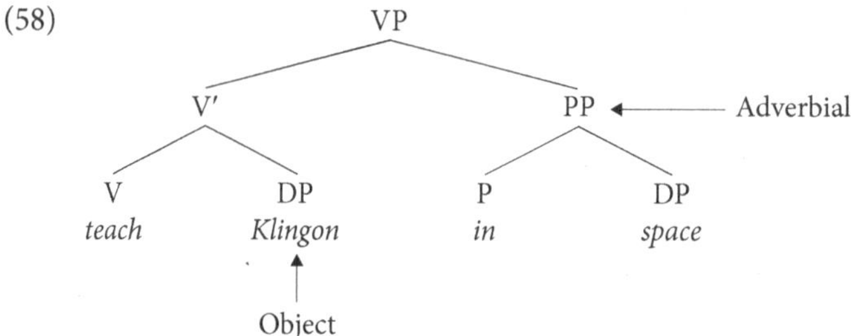

As mentioned in Section 1.3, adverbials can also be seen as Chomky-adjoined. The only difference would be that the V′ in (58) is a VP.

As mentioned, when we look at a phrase, the DP in (59), people refer to objects and adverbials as complements and modifiers, respectively. We can again discover the difference between complement and modifier by looking at who is whose 'sister'. For instance in (59) *of physics* is sister to the N *teacher* and is therefore its complement, whereas *from England* is sister to the N′ *teacher of physics* and therefore its modifier.

(59)

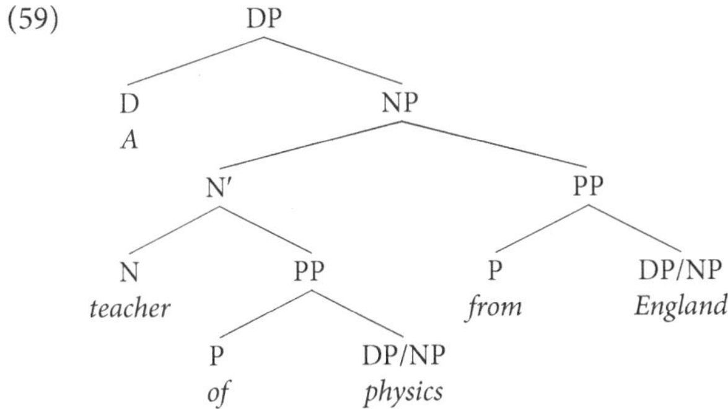

There can only be one complement but many modifiers and the order between complement and modifier cannot be reversed as (60) shows.

(60) *A teacher from England of physics.

An important diagnostic for N and N′ is that *one* pronominalizes the N′ but not the N. In (61), the N *teacher* together with its complement *of physics*, i.e. the N′, can be replaced by *one*. The N *teacher* canNOT be replaced by *one*, shown in (62).

(61)   I know the teacher of physics from England and the one from France.

(62) *I know the teacher of physics from England and the one of chemistry.

Complements and modifiers can also precede the N as in (63). Again the complement is closer to the head N and the modifier is further away. Their order cannot be reversed as (64) shows and there can only be one complement but many modifiers.

(63)

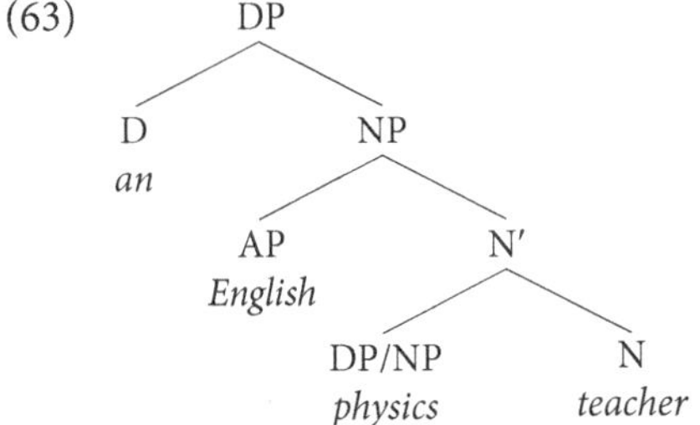

(64) *A physics English teacher.

This section has looked at functions, the subject, object or complement, predicate, and adverbial or modifier. Functions can be read off the tree and the most important is that complements are sisters to V and N whereas modifiers are sisters to V′ and N′.

5.   Conclusion

The main topics in this chapter have been phrases, sentence structure, hierarchy, and functions. The categories from Chapter 2 all project into phrases and these provide the building blocks of the sentence, which consists of a spine of a CP, TP, and VP. The CP layer links two sentences and indicates if the sentence is a question; the TP provides information whether or not the sentence is finite and, if so, what its tense is; and the VP contains the verb and its arguments, as we'll see in the next chapter.

Structural hierarchy is important for many linguistic phenomena, e.g. how to construct questions, interpret reflexives, and use negative polarity items. We ended the chapter by discussing the grammatical functions. These determine subject verb agreement and word order.

There are many other issues that come into play, some of which we have considered already. For instance, what is the role of the lexicon and how do native speakers in fact construct a sentence? In Chapter 1, we saw a model for a derivation, repeated as Figure 3.2.

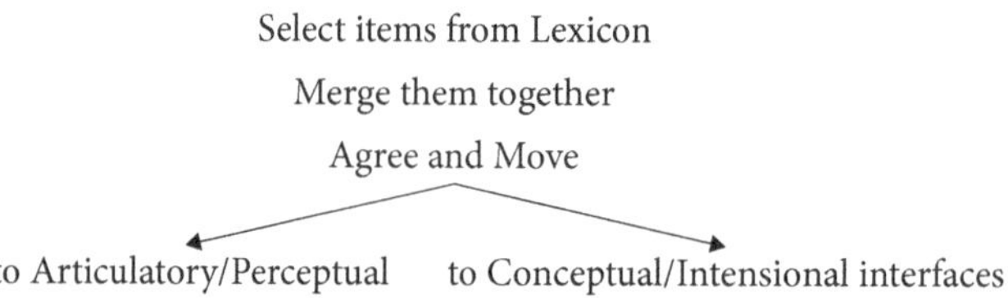

Figure 3.2 Simplified derivation

Let's look back at that and reflect on how that relates to our sentences, e.g. (35) of Section 2.2, repeated as (65).

(65)   Who will you see ~~who~~?

To form the tree for (65), we start with a selection from the lexicon: {who, see, you, T, C, will}. The T and C will have specific features for finiteness and tense which we'll ignore here. After taking elements from the lexicon, they 'merge' into phrases such as (66) from bottom-to-top.

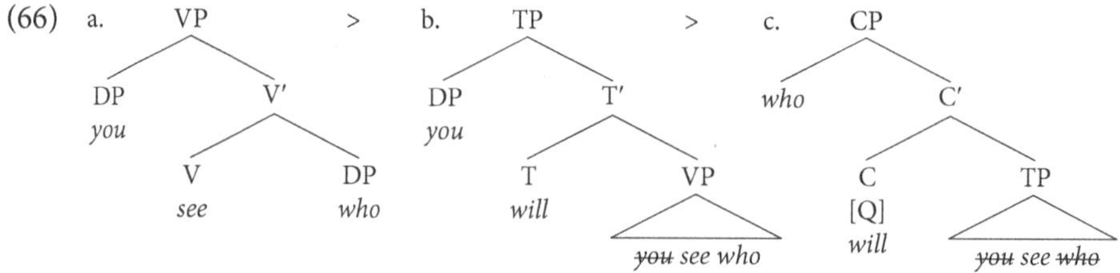

As we'll see in the next chapter, all argument DPs start out in the VP, as in (66a). Thus, after merging the VP in (66a), the T is added in (66b), and because the T in English has certain features, a DP needs to be in its specifier position and *you* is moved there. Finally, the C is merged with features that attract the *wh*-pronoun to the specifier of the CP, as in (66c). Thus, the tree is built from bottom to top in the syntax. After this, it is transferred to the interfaces and is pronounced (or signed or typed) and interpreted. That process proceeds from left to right, i.e. from top to bottom.

At the end of this chapter, you should be able to draw trees for simple phrases and sentences, find hierarchical relationships between phrases, and be able to assign functions to the phrases.

Exercises

A.   What is the name of the bracketed constituent in (1)? Why is it a constituent (2 reasons)?

(1)   They so love to [visit the elephants in Kashmir].

B.   Groucho Marx uses structural ambiguity a lot, as in (2) below. Explain in words how the PP *in my pajamas* in (2) is ambiguous, in at least two ways.

(2)   I once shot an elephant in my pajamas. How he got in my pajamas I'll never know.

C.   Which of your meanings of (2) goes with which tree in (3)?

(3)   a.

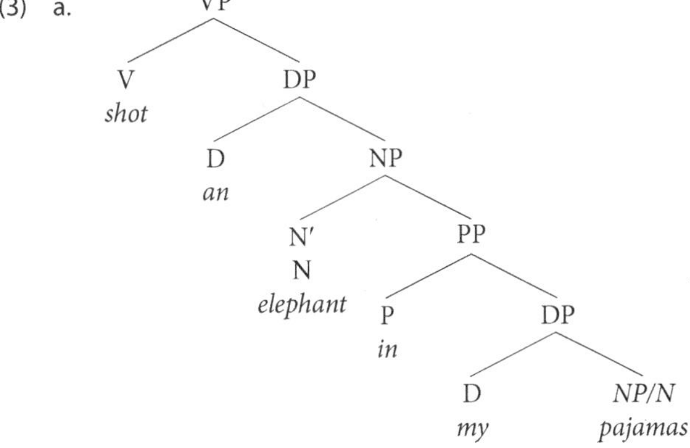

b.

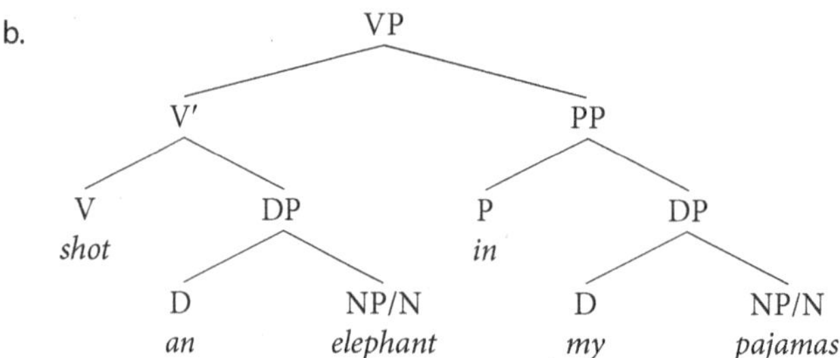

D.   Draw trees for the DP/NP in (4) and the CP in (5).

(4)   Canadian students of English …

(5)   Where did the English student live?

E.   Does *not* c-command *any* in (6)? Draw a tree.

(6)   He will not attend any festivity!

F.   In the below texts, circle the adverbials and underline the direct objects, i.e. look at the verbs.

Easier
Arizona continues to have a sunny outlook on water security during the prolonged Southwestern drought. This attitude is accurately contradictory. The state is building a sprawling Sun Belt metropolis right now but there's also an urgency about keeping millions of newcomers well-supplied decades into the future.
(from <http://www.azcentral.com/story/news/arizona/investigations/2015/12/19/beyond-the-drought-how-does-arizona-grow-from-here/76104258/>)

More difficult
The office setting may be a familiar one, but navigating its complex politics can be fraught. Some find their way by forging machiavellian alliances, others try candy to get in the good books but making the tea might represent the best path to making office life bearable. It can be tricky, but here's a five-point plan to earn the respect of your colleagues and ensure your bibitory work is fully appreciated.
(from <http://www.theguardian.com/lifeandstyle/2015/dec/08/tea-time-at-work-office-tips>)

Chapter 4

The VP

Keywords: Intransitive, transitive, ditransitive; agent, causer, theme, experiencer; durative, telic stative; unaccusative and unergative; VPISH, QP; VP-shell; the empty elements pro and PRO, control verbs.

In this chapter, we discuss verbs and their arguments. The knowledge about arguments and aspect is part of the conceptual system, as we saw briefly in Chapter 1, and interacts with non-linguistic areas. Traditionally, verbs are classified as transitive or intransitive or ditransitive depending on how many arguments they need. In this chapter, we will provide names for the different semantic roles that the arguments play and also argue that verbs have a duration, a change of state, or a state as their aspectual characterization. This characterization will determine the types of arguments a verb will have. For instance, a verb like *dance* emphasizes a certain manner and duration and therefore an Agent will be relevant but a verb like *arrive* emphasizes a change and an end result and therefore a Theme will be relevant. Verbs like *love* are stative and require an Experiencer and a Theme.

We first go into the semantic roles of arguments, also called theta-roles. Evidence will then be provided that all the arguments of a sentence start out in the VP and that one of these moves to the TP to serve as subject, which is a grammatical role. The VP will end up being split into vP and VP and all arguments will be accommodated into this VP-shell. Under certain circumstances, one argument of a verb is not expressed and we will discuss these empty elements more, having mentioned them briefly in Chapter 1.

The outline is as follows. In Section 1, we discuss verbs, their theta- or semantic roles, and their inner aspect. In Section 2, it is shown that certain arguments move to a position outside of the VP. In Section 3, a VP-shell is argued for, accommodating verbs with more than two arguments, and introducing two kinds of intransitive verbs. Section 4 examines empty arguments and Section 5 is a conclusion.

1.   Verbs and theta-roles

Verbs can be classified for the number of arguments they have. For instance, transitive verbs have two arguments and intransitive verbs have one. Verbs are traditionally seen to range from zero to three arguments, as shown in (1).

(1) a. rain, snow   0 arguments
     b. swim, arrive   1 arguments   intransitive
     c. eat, see   2 arguments   transitive
     d. give, tell   3 arguments   ditransitive

The examples in (2) to (5) show these verbs with their arguments. Verbs with zero arguments have a dummy subject in English, e.g. *it* in (2), which doesn't count as an argument.

(2) It rained and snowed.

(3) Swimmers swim.

(4) They eat mushrooms.

(5) We gave them feathers.

Rather than use the generic term 'argument,' more precise roles were introduced by the work of Gruber (1965) and Jackendoff (1972). A list of the typical characteristics of the most common of these roles is given in (6). Not everyone uses exactly the same set or name, and Theme can be further divided into Patient (undergoes action and changes), Stimulus (prompts sensory or emotional state), and Theme (undergoes action but doesn't change). I will subsume all under Theme.

(6) Agent: an animate entity that deliberately brings about the event
     Causer: entity responsible for (initiating) an event
     Experiencer: an animate entity that experiences the event
     Theme: person or object undergoing the action or prompting a sensory or
                   emotional state
     Goal: animate entity that the event is done to or for
     Result: resulting state

When theta-roles are first introduced, verbs are listed in the lexicon with their theta-roles and the number of arguments needs to be matched to the number of theta-roles in the syntactic derivation. If *eat* is listed as needing two theta-roles (Agent and Theme), two arguments will be needed and to each argument a theta-role will have to be assigned. This is known as the Theta-Criterion, a principle now applicable at the semantic interface.

(7) *Theta-criterion*
     Each argument bears one and only one theta-role, and each theta-role is
     assigned to one and only one argument.   (Chomsky 1981: 36)

Expletive subjects (*it* and *there*) and adjuncts do not bear theta-roles but some zero
subjects – we'll encounter PRO and pro in Section 4 – have theta-roles.

Let's look at the examples from (2) to (5) and a few others, all listed in (8), to see
what the theta-roles can be. In (8a), the weather-verbs have no theta-roles and a dummy *it* acts as the subject. In (8b), the intransitive *swim* has an Agent that performs the
action deliberately. In (8c), an Agent and Theme appear and, in (8d), a Goal is added.
In (8e), the subject *I* is not deliberately liking something but is experiencing something and is therefore the Experiencer. The Theme is prompting this emotion. Finally,
a Causer, Theme, and Result appear in (8f): *the storm* is not deliberately bringing
about the event (in the world as we know it) and is therefore a Causer, not an Agent.

(8) a. *It rained and snowed.*
         no theta roles
     b. *Swimmers swim.*
         Agent
     c. *They eat mushrooms.*
         Agent Theme
     d. *We gave them feathers.*
         Agent Goal Theme
     e. *I like it.*
         Experiencer Theme
     f. *The storm broke the branch in two pieces.*
         Causer Theme Result

Certain thematic roles show up in certain syntactic positions: the Agent is usually the
grammatical subject and the Theme the grammatical object and the Location may be
an adjunct. A provisional hierarchy is shown in (9), which is another principle that
works at the interface. This is an instance that used to be seen as part of Universal
Grammar but is more likely due to general cognitive constraints going back to differences in animacy.

(9) (Provisional) Thematic Hierarchy
     Agent > Theme > Location

The higher an argument is on the Thematic Hierarchy, the higher it is in the tree.

Since at least Fillmore (1970), people have thought of verb meanings in terms of
either manner/process/duration (all terms are used somewhat interchangeably) or in
terms of change of state/telicity. This characterization is known as their inner aspect
(or Aktionsart) and it is often formulated as a four-way distinction, e.g. in Vendler

(1967), Verkuyl (1972), Pustejovsky (1988) and others, and this is shown in Table 4.1. The definition of 'telic' is 'reaching an endpoint.'

Table 4.1 Inner aspect or Aktionsart

	+durative	−durative
+telic	build a house	recognize
	(=accomplishment)	(=achievement)
-telic	swim	know, be tall
	(=activity)	(=state)

Inner aspect depends on the meaning of the verb. Accomplishment verbs are really durative with an added goal making them telic. I'll therefore assume three classes, durative (with the action having a certain duration and the Agent as a central role), telic (where the action reaches an endpoint and with a Theme central), and stative (unchanging with Experiencer and Theme).

Let's look at the same examples in (8) again and see what their inner aspect is like. In (10a), the aspect is durative but not related to theta-roles. In (10b), the activity of swimming takes some time as does the activity of eating in (10c); these are therefore durative. The activity of giving in (10d) is a complex set of actions: a deliberate durative act, involving the Agent, and a telic one, involving the Theme and resulting in a Result. Liking in (10e) involves a state and breaking in (10f) a change of state.

(10)   a.   *It rained and snowed.*
           durative
       b.   *Swimmers swim.*
           durative (Agent)
       c.   *They eat mushrooms.*
           durative (Agent Theme)
       d.   *We gave them feathers.*
           durative and telic (Agent Goal Theme)
       e.   *I like it.*
           state (Experiencer Theme)
       f.   *The storm broke the branch in two pieces.*
           telic (Causer Theme Result)

There are well-known diagnostics for these aspectual categories and a few are provided in (11) to (14).

(11)   states are typically incompatible with the progressive: **I am knowing the answer.*

(12)   states are typically incompatible with the imperative: **Know English.*

(13)   durative predicates can be modified by a *for-* adverbial: *They ate for hours.*

(14)   telic predicates can be modified by an *in*-adverbial: *He reached the top in an hour.*

An (atelic non-durative) state, such as *be tall*, cannot occur as a progressive or an imperative, as (15) shows, and cannot be modified by either a *for*-adverbial or *in*-adverbial, as (16) and (17) show.

(15)   *You aren't **being tall. Be tall!**

(16)   *He was tall **for an hour.**

(17)   *He was tall **in an hour.**

Living in a non-realistic universe or using magic, these are all perfectly possible of course because their real meaning can be coerced.

There is a lot of evidence that aspect and argument structure are related and a huge literature exists on it. For instance, if an object or goal is added, as between (18) and (19), the aspectual interpretation changes from durative to telic.

(18)   He **ran** for hours/*in 5 minutes   (durative)

(19)   He **ran** <u>to the store</u> in five minutes   (telic)

If the object is indefinite or if the progressive is used, the telicity is less strong, as (20) shows, than when the object is definite and the past tense is used, as in (21).

(20)   He was eating (of) a pie for hours.   (durative)

(21)   He ate the pie in an hour.   (telic)

Section 1 has provided names for verb classes and their arguments and has argued that inner aspect is important for verb meaning. The next section will discuss the structure of the V and its arguments.

2.   Subjects start in the VP

In the previous chapter, we saw that a simple VP can be as in (22). The verb *eat* is transitive and has a Theme *the spinach.*

(22)

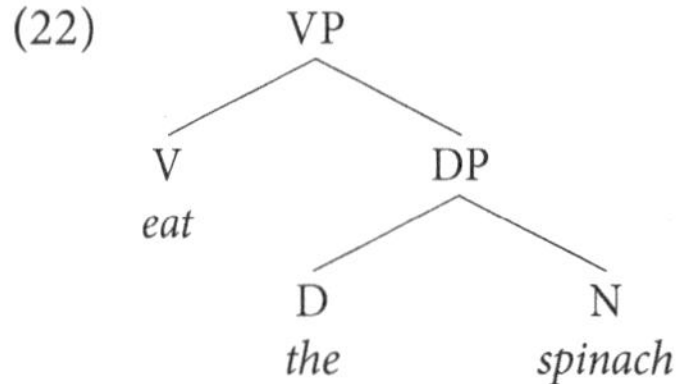

This verb *eat* also has an Agent and we know that, in English, the Agent (in bold) precedes all auxiliaries and sentence adverbs, as (23) shows, which means that the subject is in a high position, e.g. the specifier of TP, as in (24).

(23)   **The rabbits** will (happily) eat the spinach.

(24)

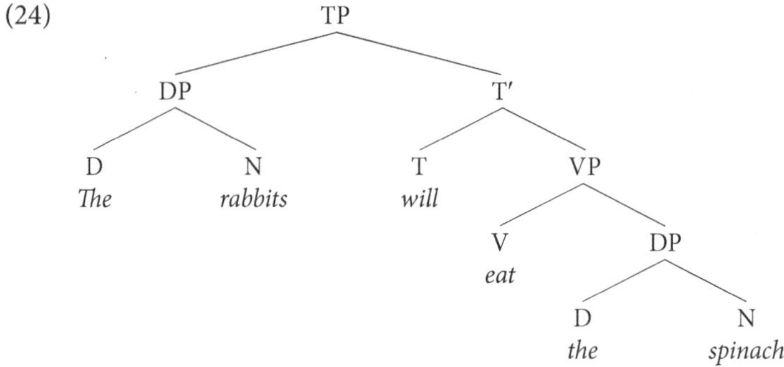

There is, however, evidence that the DP *the rabbits* starts out lower, inside the VP. Sportiche (1988), in his work on quantifier float, and Koopman and Sportiche (1991), in their work on the position of subjects, show that all arguments originate in the VP. This is the so-called VP-Internal Subject Hypothesis, or VPISH. They argue that the subject originates in the specifier of the VP and moves to the specifier of IP (not TP then yet). I have indicated this position of the (subject) Agent in (25) and also updated the I(nflection)P(hrase) as TP. The place the subject moves from is often indicated using 'strike through' font.

(25)

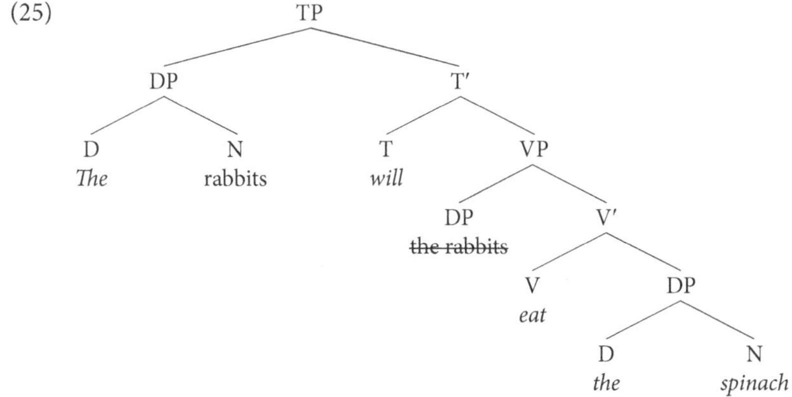

Empirical evidence for the VPISH is provided by quantifier float. Before the VPISH, it was assumed that the quantifier *all* in (26a–b–c) 'floated' to the right, away from the DP *the rabbits*.

(26)   a.   The rabbits will **all** eat the spinach.
       b.   The rabbits will **all** have eaten the spinach.
       c.   The rabbits will have **all** eaten the spinach.

Assuming the VPISH, it is now possible to see quantifier float as a process whereby the DP leaves the quantifier behind as the DP moves from inside the VP to the left. If the quantifier *all* starts out together with the DP *the rabbits*, (26a–b–c) show where the DP *the rabbits* has in fact moved from a lower specifier position to a higher one. The quantifier Q is the head of a QP with the DP as its complement. A tree for (26a) is given in (27); in Chapter 5, we'll see how to accommodate more than one auxiliary, as in (26–b–c), in a tree.

(27)

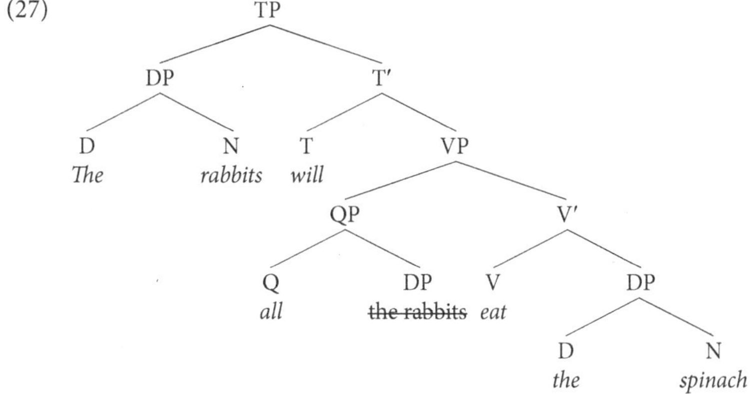

Positions where *the rabbits* are not base generated do not have *all*, e.g. (28), another indication that floating quantifiers are a good test for the position of a DP before movement to the Specifier of the TP.

(28) *The rabbits will have eaten the spinach **all**.

Not all languages need to move their subject to the Spec TP, as in (25). English is said to have a feature in T that triggers it, called the EPP-feature. Arabic and Spanish have optional movement, as well as pro-drop.

In Section 2, we have argued that all the arguments start out in the VP and that one of them, usually the Agent, moves to the specifier of the TP in English. The evidence is that the quantifier is left behind.

3.   The vP and VP

The VP-shell was first used by Larson in 1988 as a way to decompose a verb. Many verbs that have three arguments and a double VP accommodates this. Sentence (29) expresses a rolling event, the change of location of the Theme *the ball* to a resulting place. (30) adds a Causer and a Result.

(29)   The ball rolled   down the hill.
       Theme   Result

(30)   They rolled the   ball down the hill.
       Causer   Theme Result

The VP that we have used in Chapter 3 is adequate for (29) but the VP-shell is needed to account for pairs such as (30) and (31). *Make* in (31) is a causative light verb in the small v, as (32a) shows. It is optional, however; if it isn't there *roll* moves to little v, as (32b) shows.

(31)   They made the ball roll down the hill.

(32) a.

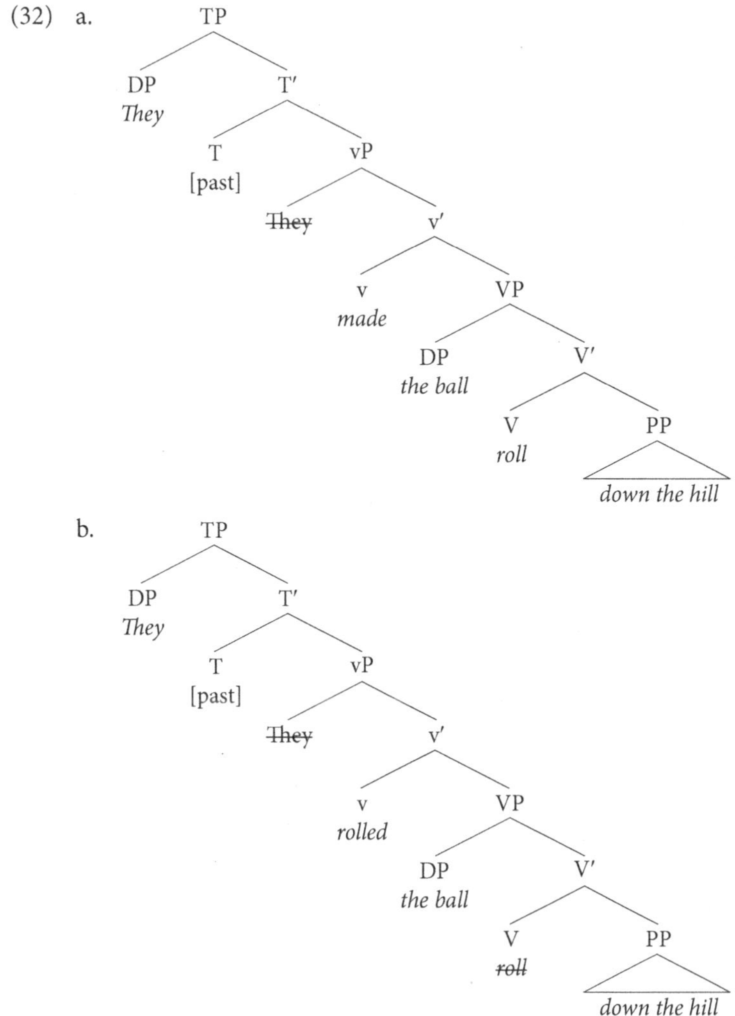

b.

The VP-shell is also used for ditransitive verbs and verbs with small clause objects (complex predicates in traditional grammar). A possible tree for the DP DP pattern of a ditransitive appears as (33a) and for the DP PP one as (33b), following the basic idea of Harley (2002). This makes the light verb *give* mean 'make X have Y' in (33a) and 'make Y go to X' in (33b).

(33)   a.

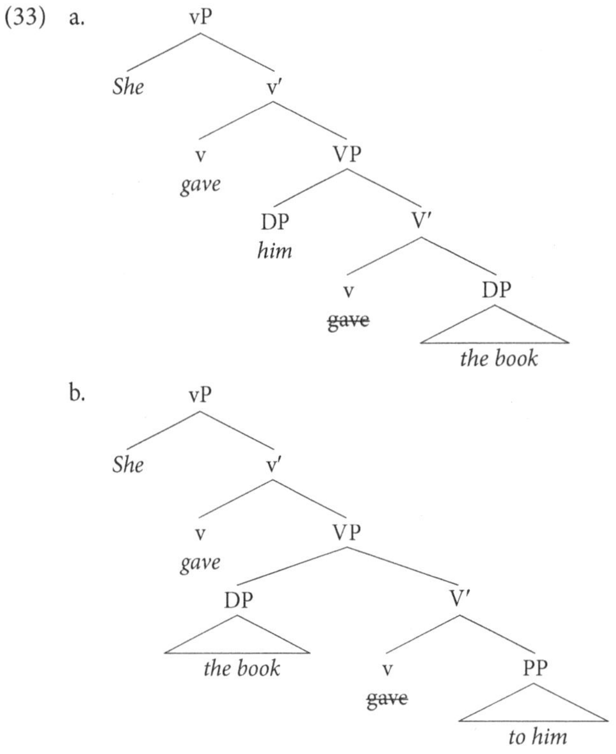

The vP-shell turns out to be insightful in accounting for intransitives. These come in two kinds, as recognized since Perlmutter (1978), with the (unfortunate) names of unergative and unaccusative. The former are typically durative (with an Agent), e.g. *dance, walk,* and *swim,* whereas the latter are typically telic (with a Theme), e.g. *fall, drop,* and *break.* The unergative verbs use the top of the shell and the unaccusatives the bottom.

Unergatives have an Agent doing something and are therefore compatible with an adverb like *deliberately,* as (34a) shows, whereas unaccusatives have a Theme as their sole argument that is affected and are incompatible with such adverbs, as (34b) shows.

(34)   a.   **She** deliberately smiled/coughed.
              Agent
         b.   * **The ice** deliberately melted/broke.
              Theme

Sorace (2000: 879) puts the difference in a structural way: "[t]he single argument of an unaccusative verb is syntactically equivalent to the direct object of a transitive verb, whereas the single argument of an unergative verb is syntactically equivalent to the subject of a transitive verb". This book will continue to think of the difference as aspectual. Typical unergatives involve willed, volitional, controlled acts, i.e. with an Agent central and a non-telic, durative aspect; typical unaccusatives involve the change of location/state of the Theme.

A list of some differences between these verbs is provided in Table 4.2. These have been discovered over the course of many years by many different linguists and some work better to predict the type of intransitive verb in one language than in another. The first five are relevant to English.

As for (a), which we've already seen, agentive adverbs, as in (34), are relevant to determine the theta-role and aspectual type.

Table 4.2 Characteristics of unergative and unaccusative verbs

	Unergative (Agent argument)	Unaccusative (Theme argument)
b.	*deliberately* is ok	*deliberately* is not ok
b.	a Theme can be added	no Theme can be added
c.	V+*er*	*V+*er*
d.	imperative ok	imperative not ok
e.	prenominal past participle not ok	prenominal past participle ok
f.	*be* + perfect participle	*have* + perfect participle
g.	Impersonal passive	*Impersonal passive (Dutch)
h.	sentence focus SV (Italian, Hebrew)	sentence focus VS (Italian, Hebrew)

As for (b), unergative verbs can be transitived by adding a Theme, as in (35). That makes sense because they don't have a Theme to start out with.

(35) a.   He danced **the cha-cha.**   unergative (COCA NBC 2010)
     b.   I wanted to dance **the part of a fisherman.**   (COCA fiction 2009)

Unaccusative verbs cannot add a Theme because a Theme is part of their inherent meaning. Thus, (36a) can only happen magically and (36b) makes *the tree* into a Causer and *a new branch* into the Theme. There cannot be a double Theme.

(36) a.   *The bus arrived **me.**   unaccusative
         Theme   Theme
     b.   The tree grew a new branch.

Related to this is another construction that is possible with unergatives in (37a–b) but not unaccusatives, namely in (37c).

(37) a.   I sneezed the page off the table.   unergative
     b.   I walked myself tired.   unergative
     c.   *I arrived the bus on time.   unaccusative

The reason is the same: unergatives do not have much of a VP and can therefore fill it up with a Theme and a Result but unaccusatives already have a VP filled with at least a Theme and optionally a Result.

Characteristics (c) to (h) in Table 4.2 are more language-specific. I will just mention them here without critical comment (see e.g. Rosen 1984 and Sorace 2002 for critique). Characteristic (c) depends on the *-er* suffix in English being used to nominalize unergative verbs with agents such as *swimmer, sneezer,* and even *cougher* but never *arriver* and *comer*. Characteristic (d) works for English as well in that *Work harder* is fine but *Arrive sooner* is not.

The prenominal participle is fine with unaccusatives, e.g. *fallen snow*, but not with unergatives, e.g. **laughed children*. As for (f), in many Germanic and Romance languages, the choice of the perfect auxiliary depends on the type of verb. Thus, in older English, Dutch, German, and Italian, the auxiliary *have* is used when an Agent is involved with transitives and unergatives and *be* when a Theme is involved with unaccusatives. An example of such auxiliary-selection from Dutch is given in (38).

(38) a. *Hij **heeft** gezwommen* Dutch
     'He has swum.'

   b. *Hij **is** gekomen*
     he is arrived, 'He has arrived.'

French still uses *être* 'be' for change of state verbs but is shifting to *avoir* 'have', compared to languages such as Italian, German, and Dutch. English and Spanish used to select *have/haber* and *be/estar* in the same way as Dutch (38) too but have lost the use of *be*, as in (38b). Using a VP-shell, where functional categories are connected to certain theta-roles, would account for the connection of the auxiliary *hebben* 'have' in (38a) to an Agent.

Impersonal passives, mentioned as (g), can be seen in (39). It is typically possible with unergatives that have control over the event but not unaccusatives (and verbs like 'stink', as Zaenen 1988: 326 argues).

(39) a. *Er   werd   gezwommen* Dutch
     there became swum
     'Swimming was going on'

   b. **Er   werd   aangekomen*
     there became arrived
     'Arriving was going on'.

The reason for this difference is that the Agent in (39a) can be lost (demoted) in a passive but not the Theme in (39b). Finally, as for (h), many languages have more frequent VS structures with unaccusatives than with unergatives.

Table 4.3 provides a list of unergative and unaccusative verbs, with the latter sub-divided into those that can alternate between intransitives and causatives.

Table 4.3 Examples of unergative and unaccusative verbs in English

Unergative	Unaccusative
bicycle, burp, cough, crawl, cry, dance, day-dream, frown, grin, hop, jog, kneel, laugh, limp, resign, run, scream, shout, smile, swim, speak, sneeze, sleep, talk, walk, work, yell.	**Alternating**: begin, burn, decrease, drop, fall, freeze, grow, increase, melt, reduce, stop, spread, widen **Non-alternating**: appear, arise, arrive, come, depart, emerge, ensue, exist, follow, occur, remain, sit

The basic structure for unergatives is given in (40). Of crucial importance is the durative aspect connected with the root. Unergatives are frequently denominal so, as mentioned, Hale & Keyser (2002: 63) argue that there is a VP with the N incorporated into the V and moving to v to merge with an Agent DP.

(40)

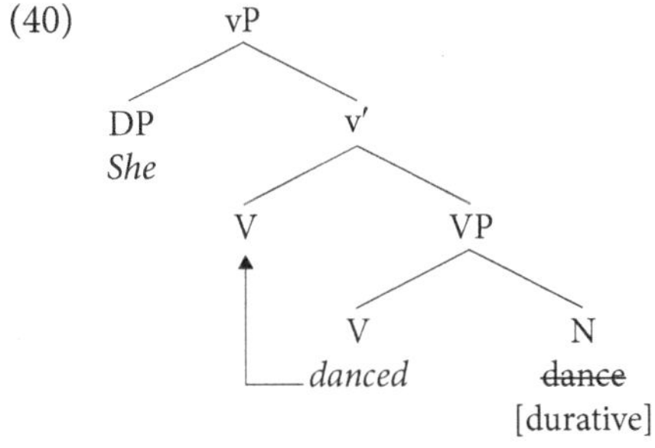

Transitive verbs have a very similar structure, with the Theme not becoming the V, as in (41).

(41)

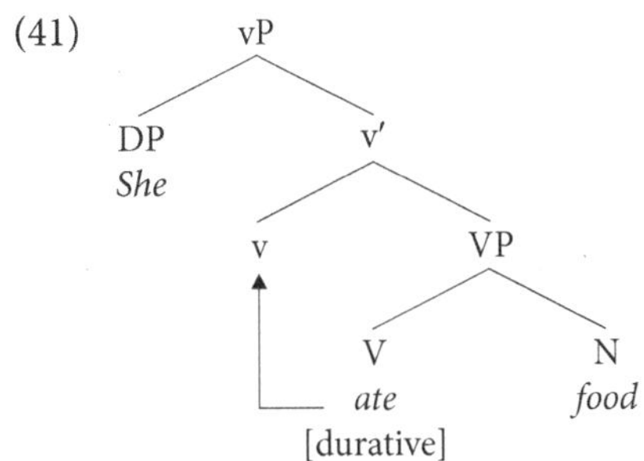

The structure for unaccusatives is given in (42) where the telic aspect is crucial.

(42)

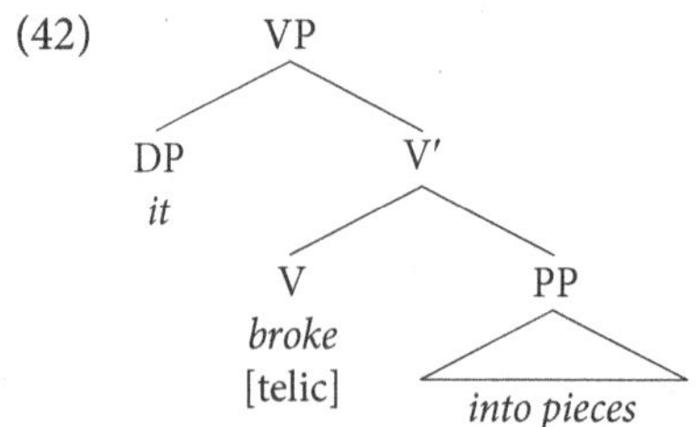

As we have seen in (32), causatives build on unaccusatives and have the same underlying inner aspect. Adding a Causer to (42) produces (43).

(43)

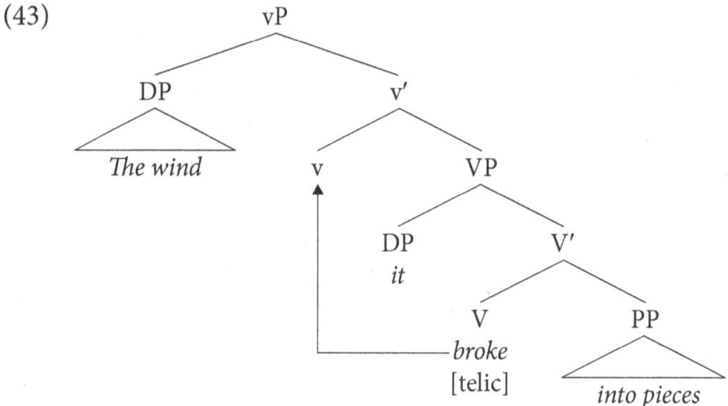

This section has introduced the VP shell, with the higher part for the Agent and the lower part for the Theme. Sometimes arguments are left unexpressed and that is the topic of the next section.

4.　Empty elements

When a word or phrase moves, it leaves a copy, which we have seen in (25) when the subject moves from the Specifier of the VP to the Specifier of the TP. In Chapter 3, we have seen copies of auxiliaries and *wh*-elements as well. Here, I want to come back to two empty elements that we have encountered in Chapter 1 that represent theta-roles, namely pro ('little pro') and PRO ('big pro').

English only has PRO and it appears with verbs, such as those in (44), that are known as Control Verbs because their complements have empty subjects controlled by the higher subject, as shown in (45).

(44)   Control verbs: *try, like, start, want,* and *expect.*

$$\qquad\qquad\qquad\qquad\qquad\qquad\text{pronounced as:}$$

(45)   They tried [PRO to leave].   They tried to leave.

A tree for these is given in (46). For reasons we won't go into, the C remains empty.

(46)

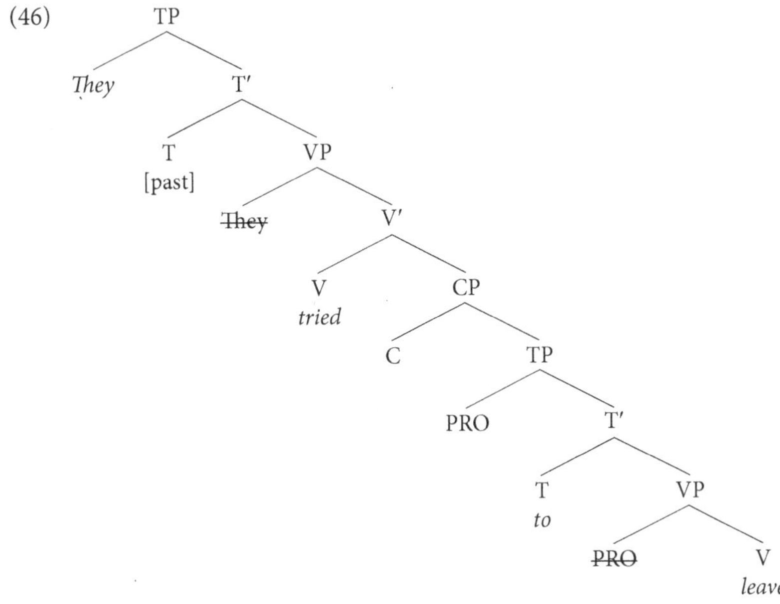

Little pro has been mentioned in Chapter 1 as a possible parametric choice. Little pro appears in languages such as Spanish and Italian where the subject can be left out, as in (47). The Spanish verb *tener* 'to have/possess' is transitive, so has two theta-roles but only one is filled overtly in (47). We therefore say that the little pro fills the other theta-role.

(47)   *tiene   un bolígrafo*   Spanish
      have.3s a   pen
      'S/he has a pen.'

Typological studies have shown that languages like Spanish are very common. Subject pronouns appear in only 30% of Dryer's (2013) language sample (some optionally and some obligatorily). Other examples of optional subjects are provided in (48) and (49).

(48)   *(Wo) he   cha*   Chinese
      1s   drink tea
      'I drink/drank tea.'

(49) *(ben) aciktim*   Turkish
      1s   hungry.1s
      'I'm hungry.'

Thoughts on what licenses pro are quite varied and depend on one's theoretical framework. Some people argue that certain features, e.g. person and number, can just appear without phonological content.

5. Conclusion

This chapter has introduced a number of new terms to describe argument structure. It has reminded us of the classes of verbs (intransitive, transitive, etc.), introduced semantic or theta-roles (Agent, Theme, etc.), and aspect (durative, telic, and state). It has also justified the VPISH where subjects start out in the VP and move to the Specifier of the TP. Finally, it has suggested a split in the VP (the VP-shell) and has divided intransitives into two classes, unergative and unaccusative, depending on what theta-role the sole argument has. The main trees to remember are (25), for a simple VP, and (32), for a split VP, or VP-shell.

At the end of the chapter, you should be able to classify verbs and try to list their theta-roles and inner aspect. As before, be able to draw trees using this new knowledge on the VPISH, the different types of verbs, and the vP/VP structure.

Exercises

A. Can you think of a transitive and ditransitive in a language other than English (e.g. your native language if you are not a native speaker of English)?

B. Make a list of five unaccusative and five unergative verbs in English (but you could do another language too). Then check if you can in fact use the *-er* with the unergative by using a corpus (e.g. <http://corpus.byu.edu/coca/>) but not with the unaccusative.

C. In the text (from <http://www.theguardian.com/science/blog/2015/dec/07/are-mammals-30-million-years-older-than-previously-thought>), identify the lexical verbs and bracket the Theme theta-roles. This is challenging!

Palaeontologists re-examined a 200-million-year-old fossil from Greenland, reigniting debate about the origins of mammals. How old are you? What if, when someone asked you this question, you answered with the age of all humans? 2.3 million years, you would say. What about all primates? Around 80 million years old. If you wanted to answer for the whole of mammal-kind, you'd find the answer depends who you ask. In November a new paper came out that stirred an ongoing debate among palaeontologists working on the first mammals and their close relatives. Early-mammal expert Professor Zhe-Xi Luo, from the University of Chicago, led a team reanalysing the fossil of a mouse-sized creature called *Haramiyavia clemenseni* using CT-scans. They found anatomical details that appear to push this little beastie out of the bushy crown of the mammalian tree, relegating it to the side branches. This has big implications for the age of all mammals.

D. Pinker (1989) provides many examples of overgeneralizations, culled from the literature. Typical examples are given in (1) to (3), all frequent in early child language. Explain these using the VP-shell.

    (1) you had a little trouble going it?   (Christy 3:5, Pinker citing Bowerman)

    (2) Kendall fall that toy   (Kendall 2;3, Pinker citing Bowerman)

    (3) Luis died my doll.   (Anne Walton-Ramirez, p.c.)

E. Draw trees, using the simple VP as in (25), for (4) and (5). Are the verbs durative or telic?

    (4) The children were painting elephants.

    (5) They read books in the evening.

F. Sentences to practice VP-shells are given in (6) to (10). Draw either VP or vP/VP trees for them, as relevant.

    (6) The bus arrived.

    (7) They closed the store down.

    (8) The vase broke into pieces.

    (9) We filled the pool with water

    (10) They withdrew the troops from East Timor.

G. Provide some sentences that include a control verb with a big PRO; no need to draw a tree.

More challenging

H. Speculate on what's happening to the verb in Figure 4.1.

Figure 4.1 "Cute him out"
F-Minus, © Tony Carrillo. Reprinted by permission of ANDREWS MCMEEL SYNDICATION. All rights reserved

I.   Try to draw a tree, using the VP-shell, for the Chinese in (11).

(11)   *Lisi na   yi   ge ping-guo gei   Elly*
        Lisi take one CL apple   give Elly
        'Lisi gives an apple to Elly.'

Chapter 5

The TP

Tense, mood, and aspect

Keywords: Agreement and case, mood and outer aspect, auxiliaries, ECM-verbs, Affix-hop, TP-adverbials, (Chomsky-)adjunction, cartographic approach, T to C and V to T movement, negation, the NegP

The TP houses information about finiteness, tense, and the grammatical subject via certain verbal inflection, auxiliary choice, and agreement (for the subject). Because this constitutes a lot of information, the T is split into Tense, Mood, Aspect, and Agreement. In this book, we use separate positions for T, M, and ASP, but place agreement in T.

Tense and finiteness are relevant throughout the sentence and are marked on C, T, and V. Finiteness is evident on C through the choice of the complementizer (*that* for finiteness and *for* for non-finiteness), tense is marked in T and visible through the ending on the auxiliary (e.g. *is* and *was*), or on the V (e.g. *walks* and *walked*) if there is no auxiliary. Note that English shows very little inflection for tense, *-s* for (third person singular) present tense and *-ed* for past tense. Auxiliaries also add modal and aspectual information. In this chapter, we look at some English auxiliaries and assign them structural representations.

The outline of the chapter is as follows. In Section 1, the content of T is presented and, in Section 2, the meanings and uses of tense, (grammatical) aspect, and mood are provided. In Section 3, we discuss the features that are shared between the subject, the T, the auxiliaries, and the verb. Then, in Section 4, movement of T to C is examined and movement of V to T (in some languages). Finally, the position of the negative can be seen through a NegP. Section 5 is a conclusion.

1.   What is in the T?

In Chapter 2 (Section 2), we reviewed finiteness, T, and auxiliaries. In English, a finite verb agrees with its subject and assigns nominative case to this subject. In the tree, the T is finite if it is marked [pres], [past], or [fut].

Take a look at (1), which is a finite, present tense sentence with a nominative subject and a lexical verb that is marked for progressive aspect through its *-ing* ending.

(1)   They are arguing about politics.

The T position contains the information about the tense (because the sentence is finite) and agreement, as in (2). The agreement is unmarked on T in (2a) until T values its features with the subject, as marked by the arrow. T values/checks by looking down before the subject moves higher. The result is given in (2b).

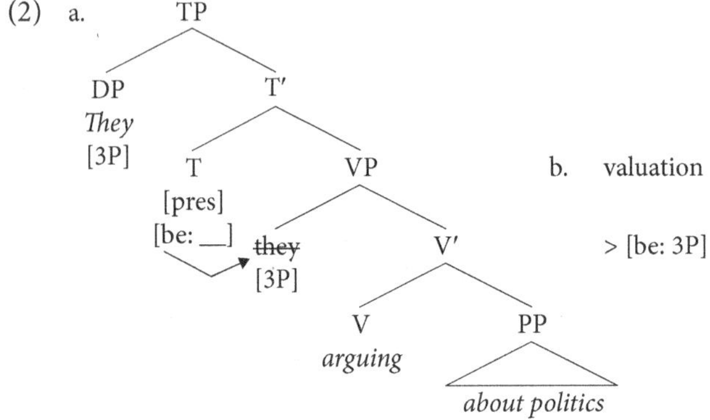

After the checking/valuation is done, the auxiliary in T is marked as [3P], third person plural. At the end of the derivation, the appropriate verb form *are* will be inserted. This is a process known as Late Lexical Insertion and adopted from the framework that is called Distributed Morphology (Halle & Marantz 1993). Once the derivation goes to the phonological (or Sensory Motor) interface, the lexical item from the lexicon is chosen that best represents the features, e.g. [be: 3P] will be *are*, not *is*. There are other ways to show the valuation; (2b) is one way and Chapter 8 shows another.

The subject *they* is unmarked for case in (3a); it receives nominative case from a finite T, indicated in (3a) as [pres]. The result is shown in (3b). At some point, the subject moves to the Specifier of TP because in English that position needs to be occupied.

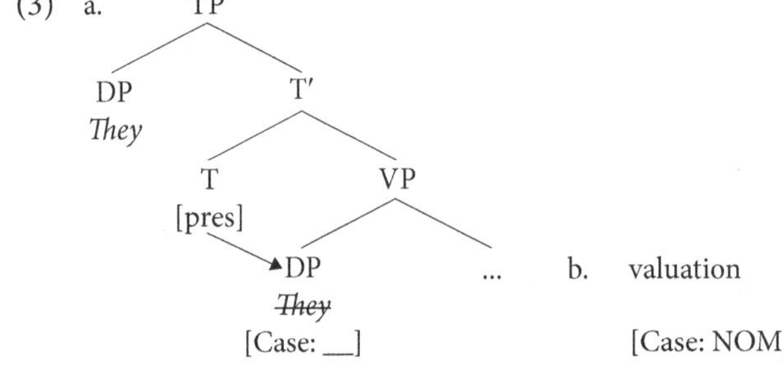

It may be that the lexicon contains an abstract feature bundle [3PNOM] that is used in the syntax and that only later *they* replaces it at spell-out. For ease of exposition, I use a real pronoun in the trees.

English has three kinds of non-finite clauses: the *to*-infinitive (*to walk around*), the present participle (*walking around*), and the past participle (*arrested last night*). A tree for one of these appears in (4), which is a subordinate clause that has to be embedded in another clause, of course.

(4)

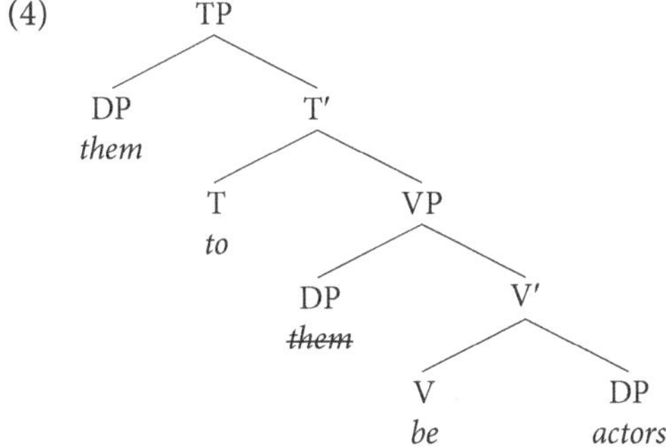

The subject in (4) doesn't receive nominative from *to* because *to* is non-finite. The only way (4) is grammatical is to place it close to another verb, as in (5). In that case, *them* gets accusative from the higher verb. These are therefore known as Exceptional Case Marking verbs, abbreviated as ECM verbs.

(5)   She believed [them to be actors].
ACC

In general, an object DP checks accusative case with the V (or v) in much the same way as a subject DP does with T. This book will not pay a lot of attention to the case of the object (but a question about it is included in the Exercises of Chapter 8).

Section 1 has discussed some of the features that we assume to be relevant to T: tense, agreement, and nominative case. We could collapse trees (2) and (3) and come to a more complete picture, namely that in (6).

(6)   a.

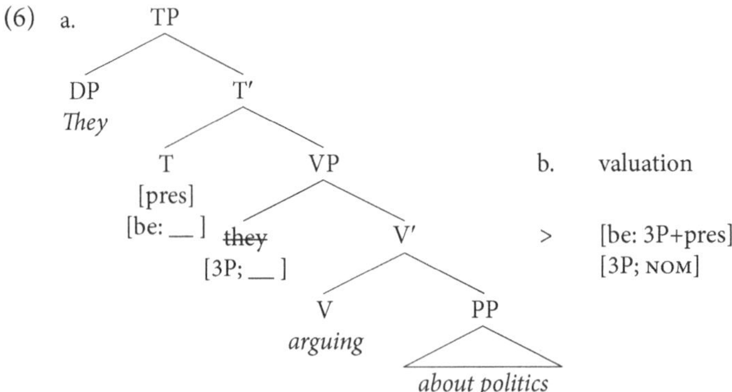

In short, the T position contains information about the finiteness and the tense of the sentence. It also mediates between the subject and the verb in providing nominative case to the subject of a finite verb and agreement marking to the finite verb.

2.   Tense, grammatical aspect, and mood

In this section, there will be an explanation of what tense, aspect, and mood (abbreviated as TAM) are and how they are interrelated. Then, we assign them positions in a tree: where before we used only a T, we'll add M and ASP.

Tense is about points in time, the present, past, and future. The latter two are the most straightforward. When something happened in the past, i.e. before the time of speaking, we use the simple past tense, as in (7a) with all verbs; a representation is given in (7b) where the event E precedes the S where S stands for the time the sentence is spoken/signed/written.

(7)   a.   They **left** yesterday.   simple past
    b.   ____ E _____ S _____
        yesterday

A future event E occurs after the time of speaking/signing/writing S; it is expressed in English with the auxiliary (*wi)ll*, as in (8a), *be going to*, or (colloquially) *gonna*. The timeline is given in (8b) where the event E follows S.

(8)   a.   I'**ll** do it tomorrow.   simple future
    b.   ____ S _____ E _____
        tomorrow

If something is happening in the present tense in English, the situation is more complex because the form will depend on the type of inner aspect. In (9a), the present tense of a stative verb is given, in (9b) that of a durative, and in (9c) a timeline is given. The S and E overlap in the present.

(9) a. She **knows** Indonesian. stative present
    b. She **is singing** (right now). durative present (progressive)
    c. _____S, E_____

The difference between (9a) and (9b) shows that durative verbs have a progressive aspect in the present tense. If we just use the present with a durative, it expresses a habit, as in *She (usually) sings.*

In Chapter 4, we discussed aspect as being inner or outer. The inner aspect is connected to the meaning of the verb (e.g. *dance* is durative) but the outer aspect expresses how a speaker thinks of the event in which the verb functions. Aspect expresses how the event takes place, not when it does. Outer or grammatical aspect adds to or changes the inner aspect.

In English, the outer aspect includes progressive and perfect(ive). In (10a), which is called a present perfect, we express both the time (present tense *have*) and that the action is still relevant, indicated by R in (10b).

(10) a. I **have read** since I was a kid. present perfect
     b. E _________ S, R _______
       childhood

There are other combinations, a past perfect in (11a), with timeline in (11b), and a future perfect in (11c) with a timeline in (11d). Timelines like these (and the above) are based on the work by Reichenbach (1947). In (11ac), the event is finished by the reference point, which is 5 pm.

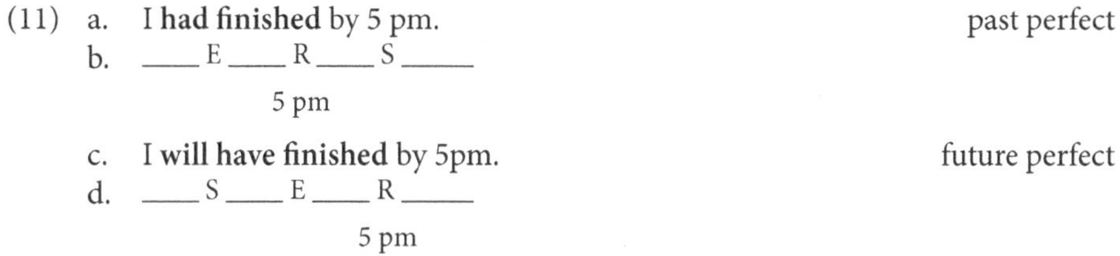

(11) a. I **had finished** by 5 pm. past perfect
     b. ____ E ____ R ____ S _____
          5 pm

     c. I **will have finished** by 5pm. future perfect
     d. ____ S ____ E ____ R _____
          5 pm

A second grammatical aspect in English is the progressive, which we've seen in (9b). The progressive aspect is used for durative verbs (although the use may be spreading to stative verbs, such as *love* and *like*). This aspect can be combined with the perfect and be in the present, as in (9b), past or future, as in (12ac), respectively. A possible timeline appears in (12b) for the past progressive and in (12d) for the future progressive.

(12) a.   He was swimming.   past progressive
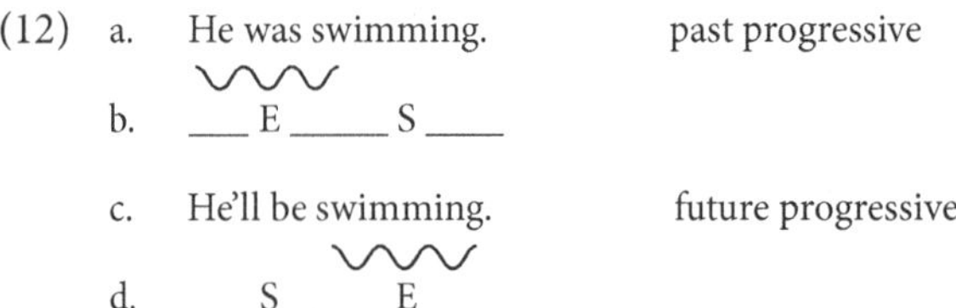
      b.   ___ E ______ S ____

      c.   He'll be swimming.   future progressive

      d.   ___ S ______ E ____

Mood adds the speaker's perspective on the sentence, e.g. if the event is likely or not. We can use adverbs, such as *probably* or *likely*, or auxiliaries. The English core modal auxiliaries are given in (13a), with some semi-modals in (13b), and some modal adverbs in (13c).

(13) a.   may, might, can, could, will, would, shall, should, must.
      b.   ought to, have to (hafta), going to (gonna), want to (wanna)
      c.   probably, possibly, maybe, perhaps, potentially, likely

Thus, tense, mood, and aspect are marked through adverbs and DPs, as in (14a), or by auxiliaries, as in (14b), or by affixes and particles, as in (14c).

(14) a.   They [possibly] saw him [last night].
                 mood   tense
      b.   I [may]   [have]   seen him.
              mood   tense + aspect
      c.   I walk[ed] around.
           tense   aspect

In the remainder of this section, we'll pay attention to the auxiliary elements and the next section looks at the role of adverbs.

Let's turn to the position of auxiliaries in the tree now. Looking at (1) again, we notice that the progressive aspect, marked on *arguing* and by the auxiliary *be,* was ignored in the above discussion. Adding those features to the tree is something we'll do in a later chapter. For now, we'll say that *be* sits in a position lower than T to indicate that it is progressive in aspect and moves to T to connect to the tense features. A tree expressing that is given in (15).

(15)

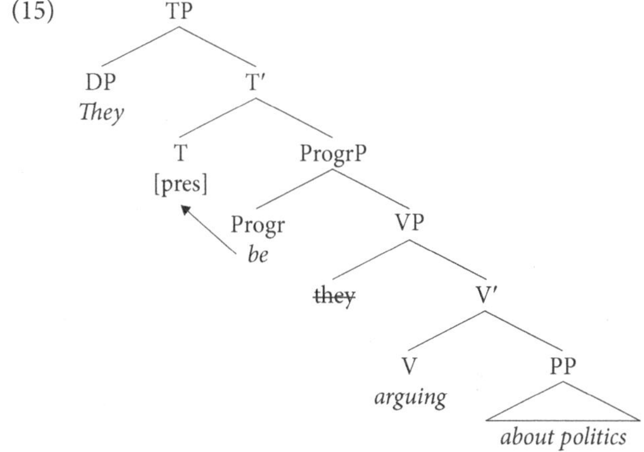

The tree (6) gives a lot of detail about agreement and nominative case; the tree in (15) is one we will typically use, where the agreement and case features are assumed but not expressed.

From (16), we see that English poses quite a challenge in the structural description of auxiliaries as well as their definition. The hyphens mark the suffixes.

(16)   He **might hav-e   be-en   be-ing** see-n (committing that crime)
          modal perfect progressive passive

The modal in (16) needs an *-e* infinitive to its right, the perfect an *-en/-ed* participle, the progressive an *-ing*, and the passive an *-en/-ed* participle. This dependence of one on the other can be seen more clearly in Table 5.1.

Table 5.1 Dependence of the affix on the auxiliary

modal + infinitive (MP)	perfect + participle (PerfP)
He might write	He has written
progressive + *-ing* (ProgrP)	**passive + participle (PassP)**
He is writing	The book is written

This relationship between the auxiliary and the verb that follows is known as Affix-hop because the affix belonging to the auxiliary moves to the next verb on its right. Affix-hop can be dealt with by features straightforwardly, which we will see in Chapter 8. For now, a sentence like (16) has a structure as in (17), where I have made the affixes visible.

(17)

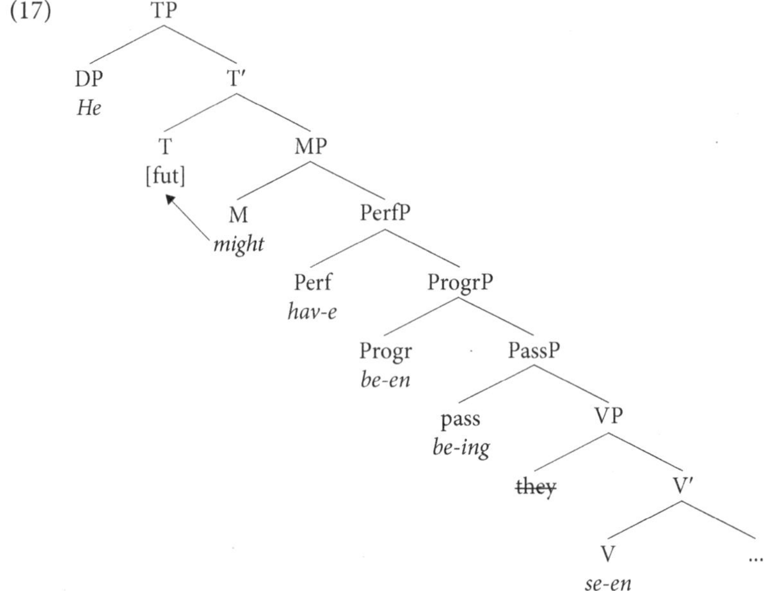

Although modals, as in (18a), display no inflection for person and number or tense (e.g. *she may*; not *she mays*), they are still considered finite and can therefore move to T in (17). Since they express irrealis mood – a not yet realized event –, I label them as future tense. They are always the first verb in the verbal sequence, as the ungrammaticality of (18b) shows.

(18) a.   He **may** be arriving late.
      b. *He has **mayed** arrive late.

Modals are divided into root/deontic and epistemic meanings, as in (19).

(19) **root/deontic**   **epistemic**
      You may go.   It might rain
      I could speak French once.   He could have left already.
      You must go.   Zoya must have done that.

A root meaning involves ability, permission, or obligation. Epistemic meanings revolve around possibility and likelihood. Palmer (2001) is helpful for more on mood and modality.

Structurally, the two kinds of modals are interesting in that the deontic, as in (20), needs an activity verb as its complement, and cannot have other auxiliaries following it, as is shown in (21), where *must* has to be epistemic.

(20) You **must** go.   deontic

(21) He **must** have gone.   epistemic

For this reason, a structure has been suggested (in van Gelderen 2003) where the epistemic is higher in the tree, in M in (22a), than the deontic, which possibly is a light verb or ASP(ect) head in (22b). Both modals move to T but, because the epistemic starts out higher, it can have a perfect and other aspectual auxiliaries follow it.

(22) a.

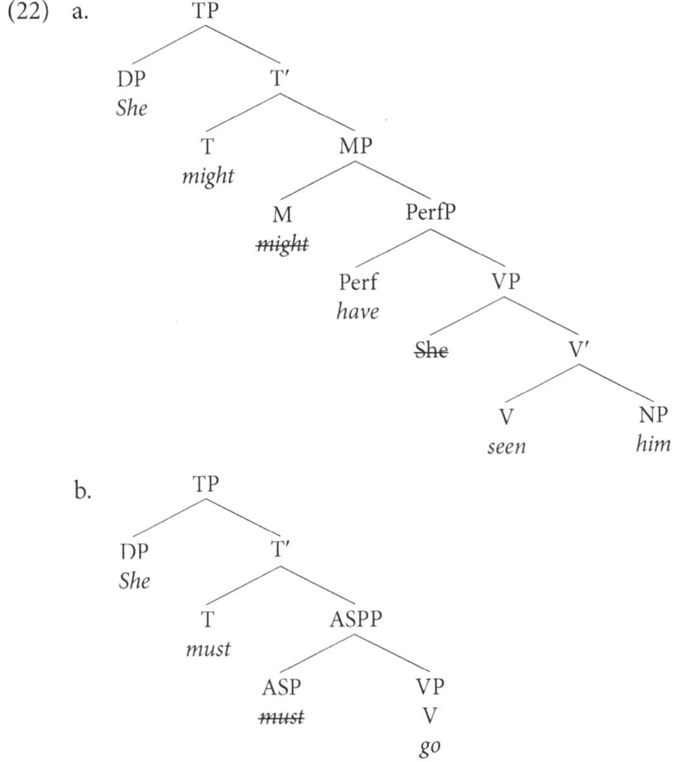

Section 2 has defined tense, mood, and (grammatical) aspect and has shown ways of incorporating the various auxiliaries into a tree structure. Be able to draw at least a tree with a TP and one other auxiliary, e.g. as in (15).

3.   TP Adverb(ial)s

We just saw how crucial auxiliaries are to the expression of aspect and mood. Adverb(ial)s add information as well and that's what this section is about. We'll see two types of structural representations.

The term adverbial refers to a function that can be filled by a PP, DP, or AdvP. In Chapter 3, we've encountered adverbials inside VPs and these can in fact be all kinds of phrases, as shown in (23a). Some of the adverbials expressing temporal meanings are found in (23b) and those expressing manner in (23c).

(23) a.   He e-mailed [quickly] [yesterday]   [out of the blue]. VP-Adverbials
                    AdvP   AdvP or DP PP
      b.   today, tomorrow, yesterday, last year, on Monday, next year, in a minute
      c.   quickly, repeatedly, for a long time

The term adverb is narrower in that a word category is meant. In the TP-layer of the clause, we also see adverbials, but they are usually adverbs, i.e. AdvPs, not PPs and never DPs. The TP adverb(ial)s are temporal, modal (taken from (9b)), and aspectual.

Table 5.2 Temporal, aspectual, and modal TP adverbs/adverbials

Temporal adverbs	Modal adverb(ial)s	Aspectual adverbs
now, then (in the past and the future), long ago	probably, possibly, maybe, perhaps, potentially, likely	again, yet, usually, often, still, already, after(wards), before

Some are ambiguous, e.g. *soon* and *once* can express either tense or aspect.

The structure for VP adverbials that we used in Chapter 3 is either as sisters to V′, as in (24a), or Chomsky-adjoined in (24b), where the AdvP and PP are sisters to VP.

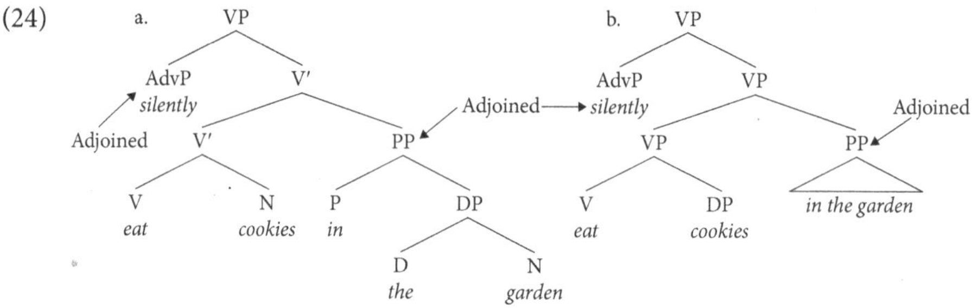

There is not much difference between (24a–b). TP-adverbials can be adjoined in a manner similar to that in (24b). This is shown in (25), where the adverb *perhaps* is Chomsky-adjoined above the VP.

(25)

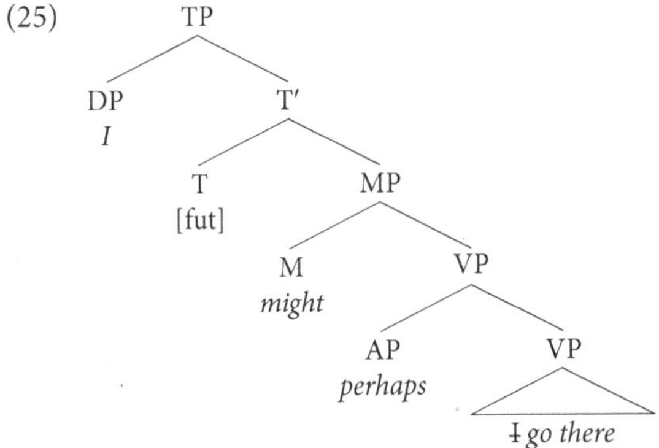

The disadvantage is that tense, mood, and aspect adverbials have a specific order and that fits better with Chomsky-adjoining them to the TP, MP, and other positions, as in (26) for (27).

(26)

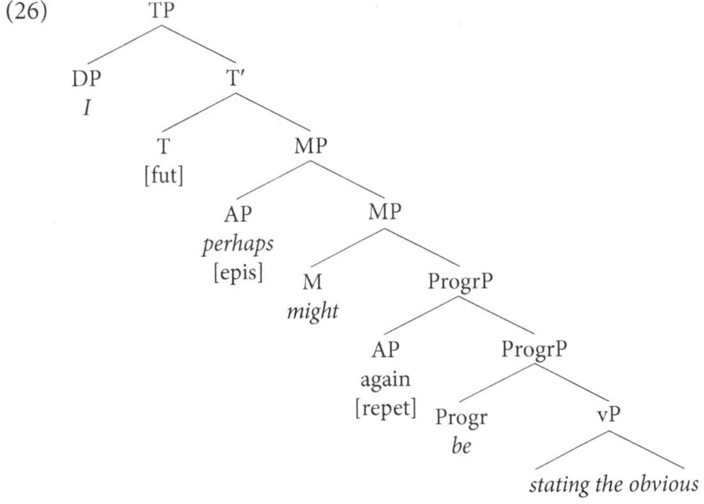

(27)   I guess I might perhaps again be "stating the obvious" and I apologise to FTers who feel annoyed by this.

(http://flyertalk.com/forum/archive/index.php/t-63529.html)

The tree in (26) is very similar to what been suggested by Cinque (1999) in (28), namely that each of the adverbs has a position in a hierarchy. In his structure, the adverbs are specifiers rather than adjoined elements.

(28)

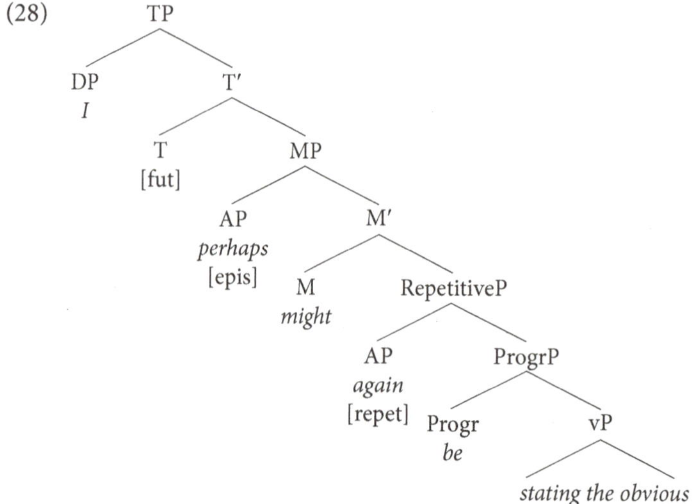

Cinque's main argument for this cartographic representation is that adverbs occur in very similar orders across languages. His TP layer looks like (29).

(29) T_{past} T_{fut} $Mood_{irrealis}$ $Mod_{necessity}$ $Mod_{possibility}$ ASP_{hab} ASP_{rep} ASP_{freq}
 once then perhaps   necessarily possibly   usually again often

(Cinque 1999: 107)

(29) shows a lot of modal adverbs. People are indeed creative with such adverbs, as Figure 5.1 shows.

Figure 5.1 "kinda sorta"
Zits: © 2010 Zits Partnership Distributed by King Features Syndicate, Inc.

There are advantages and disadvantages to (25) and to (26)/(28). The main difference is that the order in (25) is freer but that (26)/(28) accounts for the order.

4.   Movement involving T and the position of the negative

In Chapter 3, we saw that the auxiliary in T moves to C to form questions. In connection to (17) of the present chapter, I mentioned that the modal could move to T. In this section, we discuss the movement of the left-most auxiliary to T a little more and start by looking for evidence of movement into T first. From Chapter 3, we'll tacitly keep in mind that Chomsky 1995 considers head-movement as problematic. Then we turn to the position of negatives.

Auxiliaries come in many different kinds and end up moving to T in English, to connect with the tense features. The evidence is that they appear before certain adverbs, as in (30a–b).

(30)   a.   They **have often** succeeded.
  b.   They **will probably** eat less meat.   (both from COCA)

Trees for (30a–b) are given in (31a–b) respectively, where I use the tree of (28).

(31)   a.

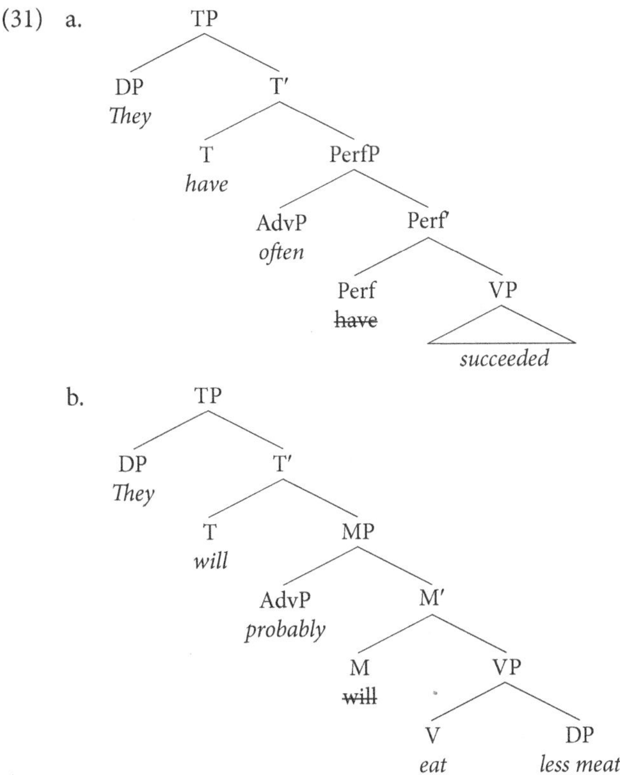

 b.

Although most people assume the highest auxiliary in a finite clause moves to T, looking at COCA, we find an occasional sentence, as in (32a–b), suggesting the movement is optional.

(32)   a.   New England missionaries, …, **often have** been blamed for putting a
              damper on the sport.   (COCA magazine 2015)
         b.   We **often have** done these types of things.   (COCA spoken 2014)

Lexical verbs do not move to T in English, as (33a) shows. They stay in the VP, as (33b) shows and get their tense features at the end of the derivation.

(33)   a.   *They **run often** more frequently.
         b.   They **often run** more frequently.   (COCA)

The lexical verbs *have* and *be* are interesting and varieties differ. In American English, *have* typically patterns with other lexical verbs in not moving to T, as (34a) shows, or to C, as the appearance of the dummy auxiliary in (34b) shows. The lexical verb *be* is different in that it always moves to T and C, as (35) shows.

(34)   a.   Presidential candidates **often have** scandals   (COCA spoken 2014)
         b.   And now the question is, **do** people **have** a plan forward?

                                                                          (COCA spoken 2007)

(35)   a.   But he **is often** out of control.
         b.   **Is** it part of our DNA whether we're happy or not?   (COCA spoken 2015)

Both *often* and *probably* can appear in other parts of the sentence and therefore the later sentences with negatives will show the difference between auxiliary and lexical verb conclusively. Earlier English did move its lexical verbs to T (and C), as (36) shows, where the verb has moved to the left of the negative.

(36)   I **speake** not this in estimation.   (Shakespeare, *1 Henry IV* I, iii, 272)

Modern English questions and negatives need to have something occupy T and, if there is no auxiliary, a dummy *do* is used, as in (37).

(37)   They **do** not want to go.

Apart from movement to T, there is also movement from T to C, as we've seen in Chapter 3. Let's take a simple *yes/no* question, as in (38). Again, in present-day English, this is restricted to auxiliary verbs but in earlier English, main verbs participated too.

(38)   **Were** they eating pancakes?

If I put the right emphasis on the words and a lot of question intonation, I could form the same question without movement, as (39) shows.

(39) They were eating pancakes???

So far, this section has outlined movement to and from the T-head. The negative *not* is positioned in the area below T and we'll look at that next.

In (36) and (37), we saw sentences with *not*. The negative in English most often appears as a clitic attached to the auxiliary, as in *don't, won't,* and *can't.* That leaves us two options, either these auxiliaries are listed in the lexicon as negative and modal, etc. or the auxiliary moves to adjoin to the negative. I'll show the movement option in (40).

(40)

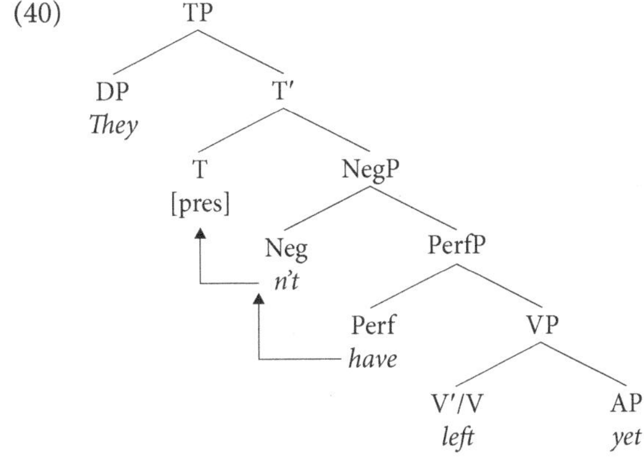

In (40), for simplicity, I have ignored the VPISH and also that the NegP and PerfP have specifier positions. What happens in (40) is that *have* needs to move to T to connect with the present tense and that it needs to take small steps from one head to another head. The result is (41).

(41) They haven't left yet.

Section 4 has provided more detail on what happens to T: auxiliaries can move to and from it but lexical verbs cannot – the verb *be* being the exception. The NegP can be seen as positioned below TP but above the other auxiliaries.

5.   Conclusion

In this chapter, we have investigated what occupies the T and TP and how the modal and aspectual auxiliaries can be accommodated by expanding this TP layer. Adverb(ial)s are relevant to marking tense, mood, and aspect as well and we looked at two alternative structural representations. Finally, we looked at how elements can move to and from T and at the position of the negative.

At the end of this chapter, you should be able to explain what finiteness is, to list the auxiliary verbs in English and to draw a tree incorporating at least one, e.g. as in

(15), to be able to place adverbials in the VP and TP, using either (25) or (28), to be able to draw a tree for a *yes/no* question and one for a negative.

Exercises

A. Provide a finite sentence and non-finite one and explain why they are finite and non-finite.

B. Circle the auxiliaries in the text and label them (a) either as just T, M, or A or (b) as modal, perfective, progressive, or passive.
(text is taken from http: <http://www.eastvalleytribune.com> (18 March 2016)).

Rural/Metro is looking to hire new employees for its emergency response force.
The company is conducting a job fair and will be looking to hire as many as 100 people across the Valley and the state of Arizona. The company plans to bring on board as many as 70 paramedics, 40 emergency medical technicians and registered nurses and 10 dispatchers. "We have a need to hire, and we're looking forward to finding some of the very best people in Arizona," said Glenn Kasprzyk, regional chief operations officer, Arizona, for American Medical Response, Rural/Metro's parent company.

C. What are the case and agreement features that are relevant in (1)?

    (1) She was meeting him for breakfast.

D. Draw trees for (2) and (3), as in (15).

    (2) They were eating pancakes for dinner.

    (3) Those elephants were soon becoming tired.

E. Draw a tree for (4) to (6), using a tree as in (28).

    (4) All Ferraris will soon have this system.   (adapted from COCA 2012)

    (5) He will almost certainly be confirmed.   (COCA spoken 2000)

    (6) There will probably always be leaks.   (COCA spoken 2005)

F. Compose an English sentence with a negative and then draw a tree.

G. Describe the position of the lexical verb in (7), which is from French. Try to draw a tree.

    (7) *Elle va   souvent à Tucson*
         she goes often   to Tucson
         'She often goes to Tucson.'

H. Think how you might draw a tree for Chinese (8).

    (8) *wo he   le cha*
         1s drink PF tea
         'I drank tea.'

More challenging

I.   What is going on in (9) to (11)?

    (9)   I should have went to Medical School at the U of A.   (overheard on ASU campus)

    (10)   What have I do?   (Chaucer, *Miller's Tale*, 3739)

    (11)   I wanna read that.

J.   In (17) of this chapter, we saw the passive auxiliary represented as a Pass head. It is also possible to think of the passive as part of the vP. If it is a v, it could signal that there is no Agent. Using this suggestion, try to draw a tree for (12).

    (12)   The book was read (widely).

Chapter 6

The CP

Mood and pragmatic roles

Keywords: (C)omplementizer, mood, complementation, raising verbs, *wh*-movement, topic and focus, CP-adverbials

The C(omplementizer) head in the CP performs many functions. It is the link between the statement in the TP and another sentence (as in *I know **that** she left*) or indicates the function of the TP in a particular pragmatic situation, i.e. as a question or a command. As a result, the C contains information on the status of a clause as declarative, subjunctive, or another mood. Certain of these moods, e.g. the interrogative in English, require that an element move to CP.

The CP can also contain topic and focus elements, which are pragmatic roles. There are adverbials that are typical for this layer; they indicate the happiness or doubt of the speaker with what the TP expresses.

The outline of this chapter is as follows. Section 1 discusses the subordinate CP and shows that its C contains mood (and tense) features. It looks at subordinate clauses in general, not all of them full CPs. In Section 2, we expand on the *wh*-movement as it was dealt with in Chapter 3. Section 3 discusses the pragmatic roles of topic and focus and Section 4 those adverbials connected with the CP layer. Section 5 is the conclusion.

1. The subordinate C

As we've seen in Chapter 2, the C-position is used for complementizers, such as *that* and *for*. The presence of complementizers shows that the TP following the C is dependent on another verb and that it is is finite (in the case of *that*) or non-finite (in the case of *for*). In this section, I review the functions of the subordinate C and ascribe mood features to it as well as to the matrix C. I also examine how verbs vary in the types of clausal complements they select.

In Chapter 3, we saw structures, such as (22), repeated as (1). The entire sentence is a declarative and I could have started with a CP above the TP containing declarative features. Most of the time, however, the declarative mood is seen as the default and not marked. The subordinate C in (1) can be left empty as well because the features connected with C are declarative. In this chapter, as in the previous one, I ignore the VP-shell since we are focusing on the higher layers.

(1)

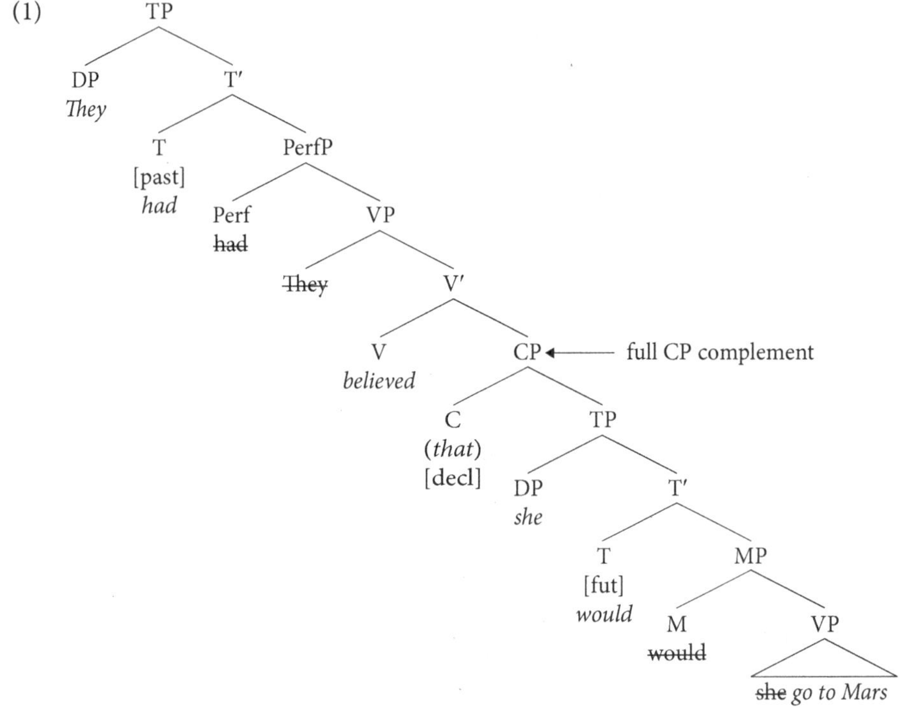

Apart from full CP complements, as in (1), we have seen in the previous chapter that English has what is called ECM (Exceptional Case Marking) verbs, as in (2), whose complement lacks the CP layer altogether.

(2)   I believe [him to be totally innocent].   (COCA 2007 CBS)

ECM clauses are so called because the accusative subject of the infinitive, *him* in (2), doesn't get case from *to be totally innocent,* i.e. the verb it is the subject of, but from the verb in the higher clause. A tree is given in (3).

(3)

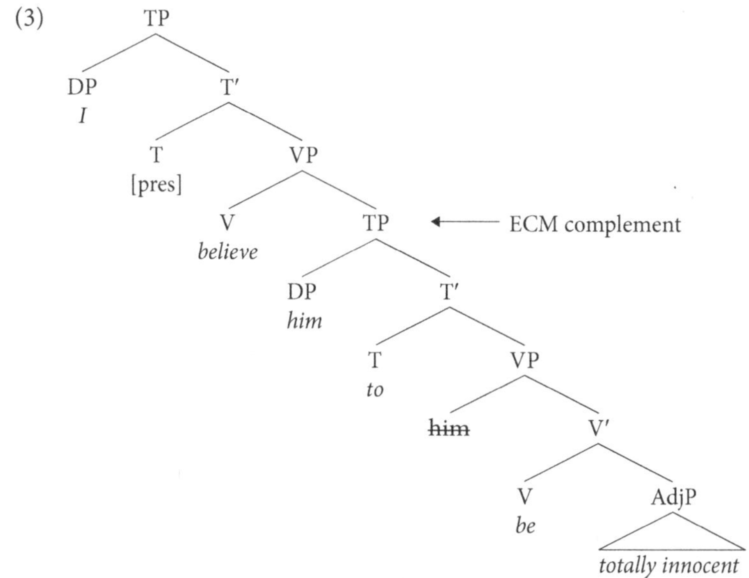

The structure for the verb *believe* is different from that of verbs like *want* in (4a). The latter, unlike *believe*, has an optional *for* that assigns accusative case, as shown in (4b). That means there is a CP complement. Many speakers find *for* superfluous though grammatical. The presence of the CP boundary makes passivization ungrammatical, as (4c) shows.

(4)   a.   I want him to be totally innocent.
      b.   I want **for** him to be totally innocent.
      c.   *He is wanted to be totally innocent.

A tree for (4b) is shown in (5).

(5)

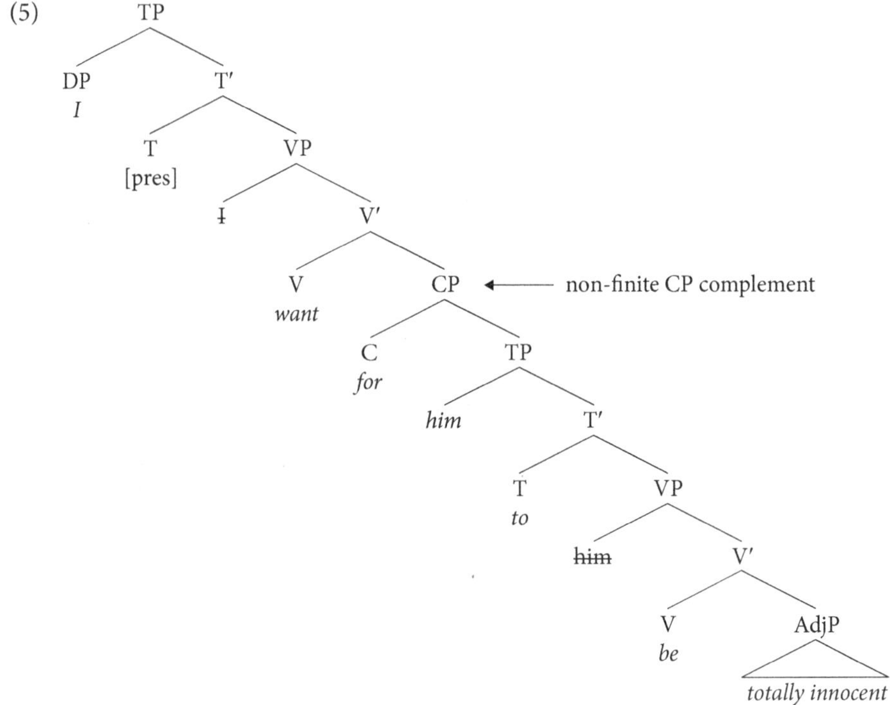

Because *believe* lacks the C *for*, as shown by the ungrammatical (6a), it also lacks a CP boundary in (3) and can therefore passivize the subject of its embedded clause, as (6b) shows.

(6)   a.   *I believe [for her to be innocent].
       b.   She is believed [to be still in New Zealand].   (COCA 1995 ABC 20/20)

Depending on the type of complement the two clauses are more or less dependent on each other, as shown in Figure 6.1.

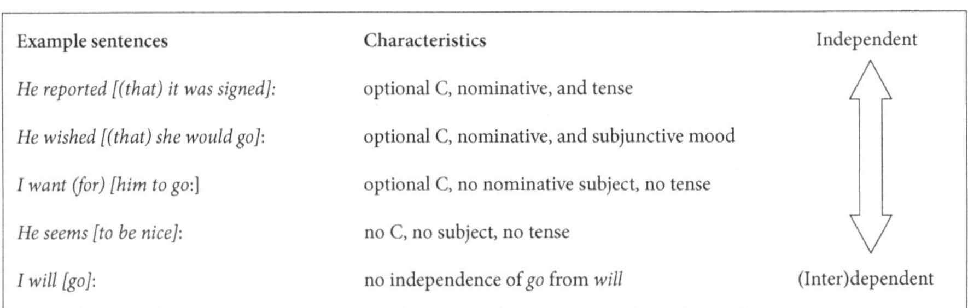

Example sentences	Characteristics	Independent
He reported [(that) it was signed]:	optional C, nominative, and tense	
He wished [(that) she would go]:	optional C, nominative, and subjunctive mood	
I want (for) [him to go:]	optional C, no nominative subject, no tense	
He seems [to be nice]:	no C, no subject, no tense	
I will [go]:	no independence of *go* from *will*	(Inter)dependent

Figure 6.1 Degrees of clausal (in)dependence

To account for these options, we'll argue that complementizers are first of all markers of realis (declarative/indicative) or irrealis (subjunctive) mood. The CP that is chosen by *want*, for instance, is irrealis mood because the event hasn't been realized. In English, the subjunctive can be marked through modals, such as *would* or *should*, or past (*I wish he were here*). This is a complex area and we are just scratching the surface.

Sentences such as (6b) are referred to as raising constructions, because their subjects 'raise' from one subject position to another. Raising also happens with a special class of verbs, verbs that have no Agent of their own, such as *seem, appear*, and *be likely* and that have either a TP or CP complement. Raising only occurs in the TP complement scenario, as in (7a), because the CP boundary stops it, as in (7b), and an expletive *it* is used instead to fill the subject position. A raising tree is given in (7).

(7) a.   He seems [~~he~~ to have left].   TP complement
     b.   It seems [that he has left].   CP complement
     c.

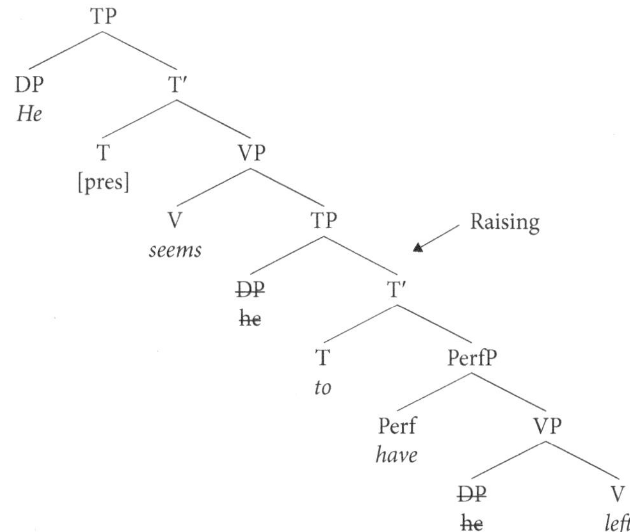

In previous chapters, we encountered ECM and control verbs and we have just added raising verbs. Examples of the different kinds of clausal complements appear in Table 6.1; note that some verbs can have more than one kind of complement.

The embedded clauses in (1), (3), and (5) are objects. In Chapter 3, (23) and (24) show that clauses can also function inside other clauses with the functions of subject or adverbial. Adverbials have very specialized Cs depending on the function of the adverbial as temporal, aspectual, or causal. In Chapter 2, we encountered a few complementizers. Table 6.2 adds to this selection where some are heads (e.g. *after, as*) and others are specifiers (e.g. *how, whether*).

Table 6.1 Clausal complements

	Verbs	Sentences
Full CP	*say, suggest*	*He said that she left.*
For-CP	*want, expect*	*They wanted (very much) for us to do our homework.*
Control CP	*try, like, start*	
	want, and *expect*	*I want PRO to go.*
ECM	*believe, consider*	*She considers him to be nice.*
Raising	*seem, appear, be likely*	*He seems to be nice.*

Table 6.2 English Cs for Adverbial clauses

after, (al)though, as, because, before, how, if, in case (that), in order that, in that, lest, like, now that, once, provided (that), so (that), (rather) than, till, unless, until, when, whenever, where(as/ever), whether, while, whilst, why, yet

Section 1 has looked at the content of the C in more detail and has also shown that the complementizer *that* may optionally be absent, as in (1), but that the CP remains. The CP is obligatorily lacking in complements to ECM and raising verbs, as in (3) and (7c), respectively.

2.   *Wh*-movement

As briefly discussed in Chapter 3, *wh*-movement occurs in English when we ask a content question. This movement involves a phrase that fronts to another phrase position inside the CP. Some languages (Japanese, Chinese, Indonesian, etc.) do not have this movement.

   Wh-movement explains the accusative case on *whom* in (8) in prescriptive/formal varieties of English because *whom* starts out as the object of *hurt*. It also accounts for the ambiguity of *when* in (9) because *when* could originate as adverbial to either *say* or *hurt*.

(8)   **Whom** did he hurt?   Formal variety

(9)   **When** did the boy say he hurt himself?   Ambiguous

Let's start with the theta-roles in (8): the verb *hurt* has an Agent (*he*) and a Theme (*whom*). If (8) was not a question, the order would be Agent, V, and Theme. To draw a tree for (8), we start with the VP, as in (10a).

(10a)

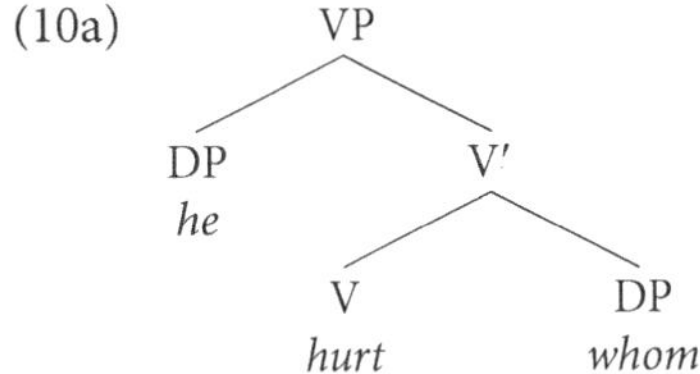

To this, we add, i.e. merge, the T and have the subject *he* move to Spec TP and then we merge the C with question features, as in (10b). Once the C is added, an auxiliary moves to C, and the *wh*-pronoun moves to the specifier of the CP.

(10b)

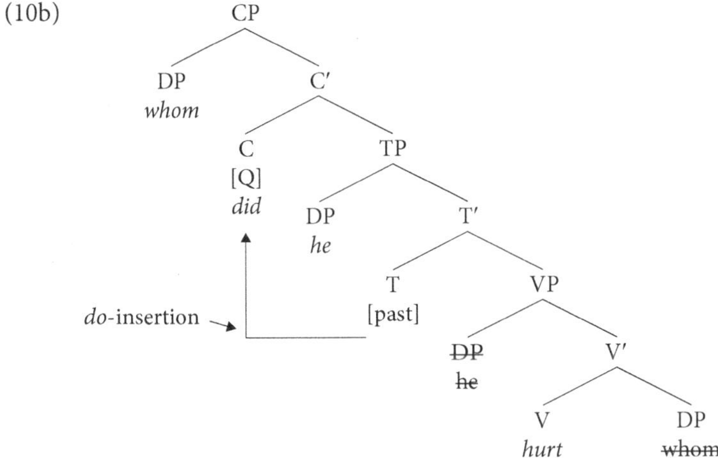

That *whom* is the object explains the *-m* for the accusative. This ending is rarely heard in spoken English, however. (10) also shows that *do* is used if no other auxiliary is present.

Since (9) is ambiguous, we need two trees, (11) and (12), where I ignore the VPISH for reasons of space.

(11)

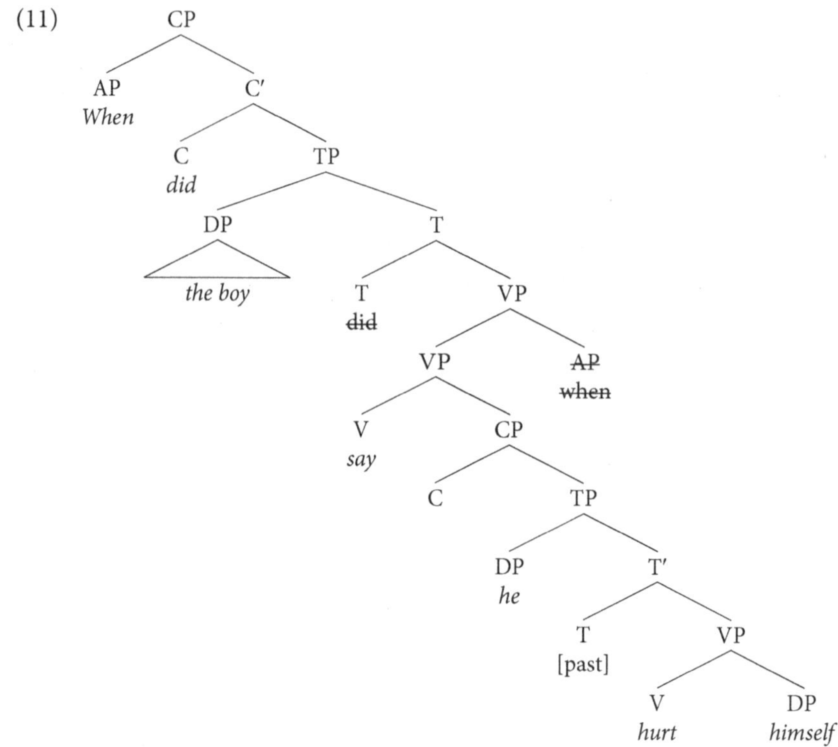

(12)

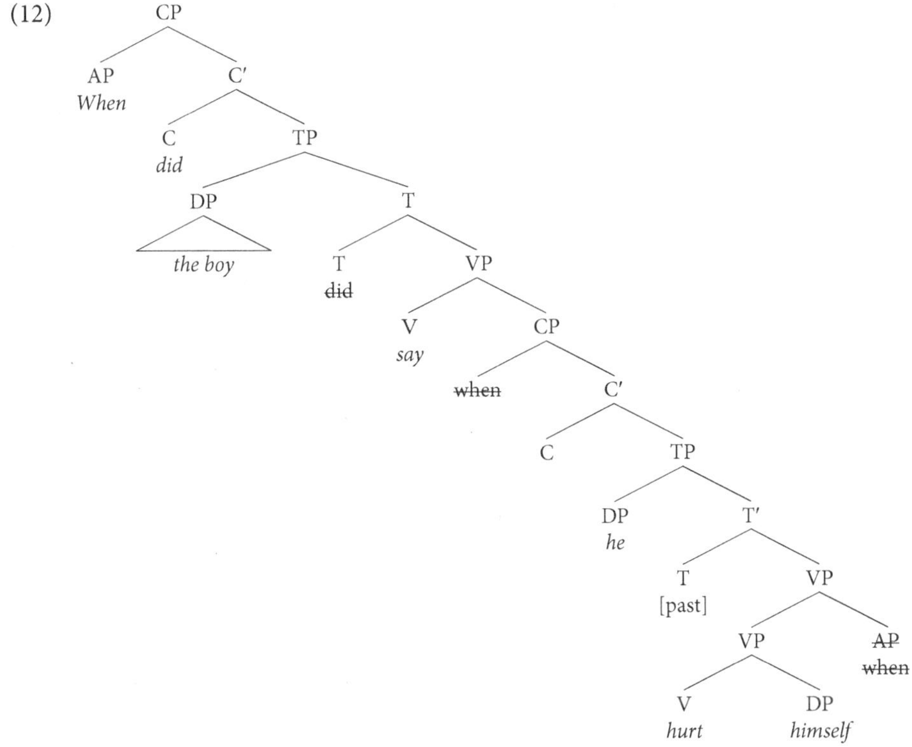

In (11), *when* is extracted from the main clause, and the sentence means 'when did he say …', whereas in (12), *when* is extracted from the subordinate clause, and the sentence means 'when did … he hurt himself'. In (12), *when* moves via the intermediate CP before moving to the topmost CP. We know that movement takes place in small steps because of the ungrammaticality of certain sentences, e.g. (1b) in Chapter 1: if something else is in the intermediate specifier of CP, the sentence is ungrammatical.

In addition to not being able to move an element very far (sometimes called the locality constraint), we cannot move a *wh*-phrase out of certain CPs. Clauses we cannot extract from are called islands because nothing can 'get off' them. Noun complements and relative clauses are famous for being islands, as has been noted since Ross (1967). In (13), extraction of the *wh*-pronoun from the CP is possible because the CP is an object clause but, in (14) and (15), it is not because the CP is a complement to a noun and a relative clause, respectively.

(13)   What did I hear [that she said ~~what~~]?

(14) *What did I hear the rumor CP[that she said ~~what~~]?

(15) *Who did they meet the man [that knows ~~who~~]?

Islands have received various explanations. One account is that the *wh*-element cannot cross two boundaries, such as the DP, CP, TP, in one step. This accounts for the multiple steps in (12): going without the intermediate step would cross a TP, CP, and TP!

I'll show these boundaries for the noun complement in (14), where the first step to the Spec of CP is grammatical (crossing only on TP) but the second is not (crossing a DP and TP), as shown in (16).

(16)   *What did TP[I hear DP[the rumor CP[~~what~~ that TP[she said ~~what~~]]]]

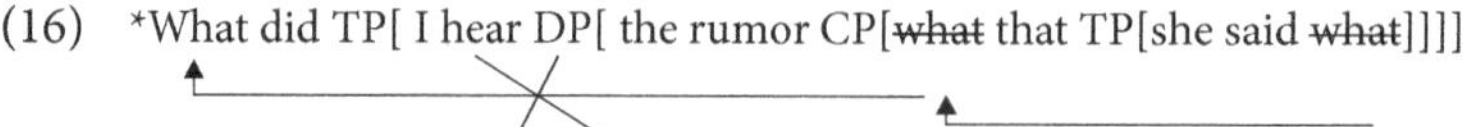

This way of formulating the constraint on movement is known as subjacency.

In the current theory, we account for the ungrammaticality of (14) and (15) through phases. The vP and CP are phases and therefore *what* is inaccessible for the Q-feature in the C to attract it. For our purposes in this chapter, it is enough to remember islands such as those in (14) and (15) with a possible explanation as in (16).

3.   Topic and focus

This section explains the difference between topic and focus and shows that certain pragmatic roles are placed in special areas of the clause, also known as the left-periphery or the split CP.

The main difference between topic and focus is providing old information and new information, respectively. Topics are known entities, e.g. the speaker is familiar with *that guy* in (17). They are definite and may have a pronoun double in the main clause, *him* in (17).

(17)   **That guy**, I hate **him**.

A focus is a new, unknown element, e.g. *what* in (18a) and *cookies* in (18b). It provides the answer to a *wh*-question, and need not move to the left. In fact, in English, the focus is often last.

(18)   a.   Question   **What** did you bring yesterday?
       b.   Answer   I brought **cookies**.

Putting the answer to (18a) in a typical topic position is pragmatically strange, indicated by a # in (19).

(19)   Answer to (18a)   #Cookies, I brought them.

(Certain) topics in English can be preceded by *as for*, as in (20), and focus by *only*, as in (21). Focus phrases also appear in a cleft, as in (22), or in a pseudo-cleft, as in (23).

(20)   **As for me,** I am rooting for my beloved Red Sox to win the World Series.
(https://www.was.org/Usas/USChapter_files/Newsletter/October04.pdf)

(21)   I brought **only cookies!**

(22)   It was **cookies** I brought.

(23)   What I brought was **cookies.**

Topics are either base generated in the CP-layer or moved there but focus-elements are always moved.

The final distinction between topic and focus is the word order. The topic doesn't bring about movement of the verb to the CP-layer, as (24) shows, but the focus *never again* does, as in (25), because the auxiliary *will* moves to C.

(24)   **Bees,** I like them in my garden.

(25)   **Never again** will I write a poem that sounds like that.   (COCA academic 2010)

Thus, the focus in (25) and the *wh*-element in (26) have a similar position which we turn to next.

(26)   **Who** will I see?

Rizzi's (1997) expanded CP projection is given in (27); it accommodates all the material appearing on the left edge of the sentence. The Force indicates the type of sentence (e.g. declarative) and the Fin the finiteness. The Topic accomodates *bees* in (24) and the Focus incorporates either the focus *never again* in (25) or the *wh*-element in (26).

(27)   …Force … (Topic) … (Focus) … Fin … TP   (adapted from Rizzi 1997: 288)

Sentences such as (28) prove that the Topic precedes the Focus Phrase but many English speakers don't like combinations of topic and focus phrases; (28) appears in Radford (2009b: 284), and (29) is its structure (where the force is left empty). The *wh*-pronoun *how* appears in the specifier of the FocP, as just mentioned.

(28)   That kind of behavior, how can we tolerate in a civilized society?

(29)

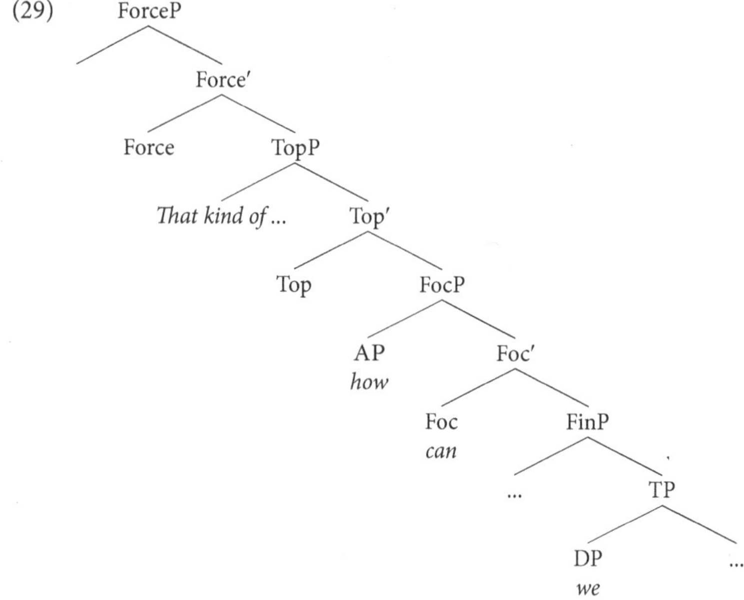

Many speakers find the sentence improves if *it* is added after *tolerate*, clearly indicating that *that kind of behavior* is a topic by doubling it.

If you are a speaker of (American) English who only places either a focus or topic to the left of the subject, you may only need a CP, as shown in (30a) for a topic and (30b) for a focus.

(30)   a.

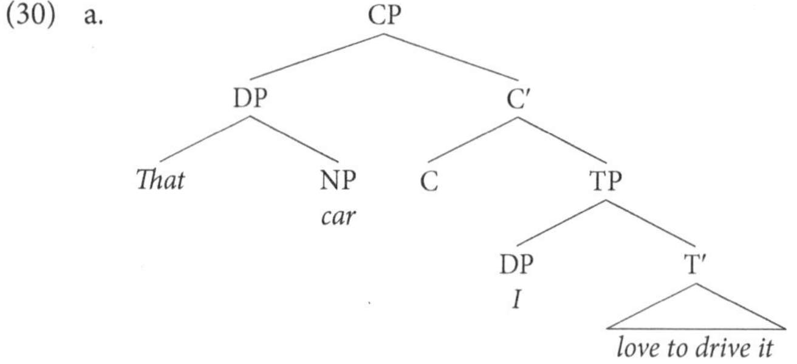

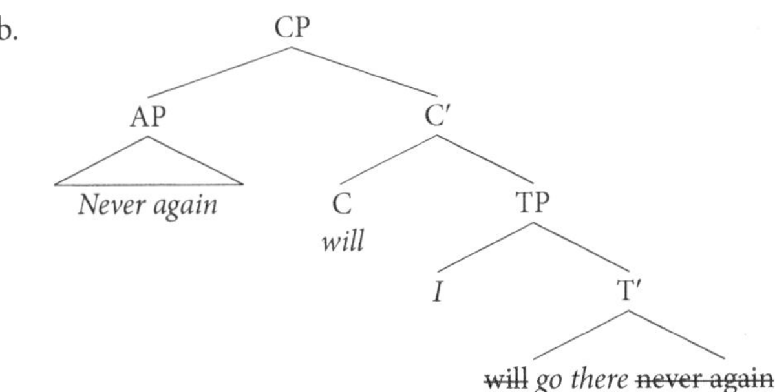

In this section, we have seen topic and focus elements that are in the left part of the sentence. It is generally agreed that CPs need to be split to accommodate these elements but how much is still a matter of debate; (29) is one suggestion but it is possible to not split the CP, as in (30), at least for some speakers of American English.

4.   CP adverb(ial)s

In addition to sentence type, topic and focus, mood adverb(ial)s need to be accommodated in the CP: speech act adverbs (*frankly, honestly*), evaluatives (*(un)fortunately*), evidential adverbs (*allegedly, evidently*), and modal affixes in certain languages. We'll look at that in this section.

The full range of the CP-adverbs is given in (31). I have added the epistemic TP-adverb as well.

(31)   Mood $_{speech\ act}$ Mood $_{evaluative}$ Mood $_{evidential}$ Mod $_{epistemic}$
     frankly   fortunately   allegedly   probably

(from Cinque 1999: 106)

Testing the compatibility of these adverbs with topics and focus, one finds the odd (32) and, testing them with each other, the ungrammatical (33).

(32) ?Frankly, those books, he should have read (them) before class.

(33) *Frankly, surprisingly, he read those books.

(32) is somewhat acceptable to native speakers which means that the speech act adverb *frankly* is in the ForceP and *those books* in the TopP. (33) presents a problem in Cinque's approach, since the speech act adverb *frankly* is higher in the tree than the evaluative, evidential adverb *surprisingly* but, unexpectedly, the two cannot occur together in (33). The adverbials in (31) all express a particular mood of the speaker and therefore only one of these can be present.

As (34) and (35) show, adverbials and topics again co-occur but the restriction on multiple CP-adverbials also holds for subordinate clauses as I didn't find any examples in COCA.

(34) I actually think **that fortunately** with all the different media that we have, people have the choice of both of those. (COCA 2000 CNN)

(35) McCain: Oh, I think **that frankly** any person who's the vice presidential nominee, it's his job, his or her job to get along with – with the nominee.

(COCA 2000 ABC)

In (34) and (35), the adverbial precedes a topic, which in the case of (35) is actually a left dislocated topic repeated by *his* in the main clause. (36) provides a tree for (35).

(36)

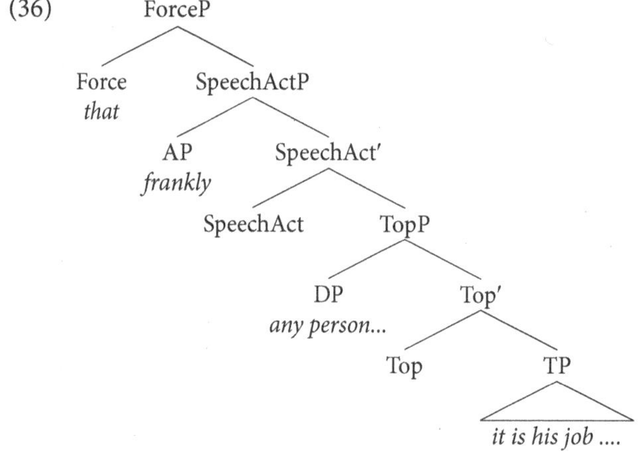

This section has considered the interaction between topicalized elements and CP adverbials which all have to be housed in the CP. Topics do appear with other adverbials but only one CP-adverbial can be used at a time.

5. Conclusion

In this chapter, we have looked at the CP more carefully and argued for an expanded version to include mood features in the C, topic and focus phrases in special areas of the CP, and CP Adverb(ial)s.

After finishing this chapter, you should be able to discuss the relevance of the CP and explain what topic and focus are. You should be able to draw a tree for an embedded clause, as in (3) or (5) and for a *wh*-question, as in (10).

A. In the text below (from <http://www.bbc.com/news/world-us-canada-35203666>), underline the complementizers and put brackets around the embedded clauses.

A Canada-bound airliner was forced to make an emergency landing after severe turbulence injured 21 passengers, including three children, officials said. The Air Canada flight from Shanghai to Toronto was diverted to Calgary after the turbulence hit. Eight passengers suffered neck and back injuries and 13 more were taken to hospital for observation. The injured were in a stable condition, an emergency services spokesman said. Bing Feng, a passenger, described hearing "lots of screaming" as the plane became "like a rollercoaster". Even enthusiastic fliers can get nervous when there is some chunky turbulence around. But although people can get hurt if they aren't strapped in, turbulence doesn't crash airplanes. Lots of things can cause turbulence, but pilots can often predict when it's coming, so they can either avoid it or put on the fasten seat-belt signs. And aircraft are built to withstand even the worst excesses of mother nature. Wings are bent until they snap, hulls are tested by attacking them with artificial lightning strikes. In the most extreme examples, turbulence could potentially damage an aircraft, but it won't knock it out of the sky.

B. Draw trees for (1) and (2).

(1)   I wonder if they'd like to go.

(2)   The monster considered them to be nice.

C. When children produce (3) and (4), what may they be doing?

(3)   Is I can do that?

(4)   Does it doesn't move?

D. Discuss the structure of (5) and (6).

(5)   Who did he say she talked with

(6)   He appeared to have no way to reach it (COCA).

E. Find a grammar (either in the library of on the internet) of a language that you don't know (and try to avoid Spanish or German) and, on the basis of the information in the grammar, describe how *Wh*-Questions are formed. Try to draw a tree for one.

F. Draw a tree for (7).

(7)   Frankly, did they look at the gentleman from Maryland?   (Congr. record V 149 Pt 10)

G. Decide what type of verbs, raising or control, the main clause verbs are.

(8)   They managed to open the door.

(9)   We are planning to leave soon.

(10)   My goldfish tends to eat too much.

(11)   We intend to do that soon.

(12)   It is threatening to rain.

(13)   We came to understand their point of view.

(14)   I happened to be doing that anyway.

(15)   The elephants hope to paint again soon.

Chapter 7

The Determiner Phrase

Keywords: Determiner, D head, demonstrative, specifier of DP, hierarchy of adjectives, N-to-D, theta-roles inside the DP

This chapter is about the Determiner Phrase, or DP. So far, we have just assumed the DP is a structure with a D head and an NP complement. In this chapter, we'll see that it can house additional elements. The English DP includes information on number and definiteness. In more complex DPs, we also see a variety of theta-roles that can be identified.

The outline is as follows. Section 1 outlines the simple DP with articles in the head D and demonstratives and possessives in the specifier position. Section 2 adds adjectives and discusses them as we have adverb(ial)s: are they adjoined freely or do they have designated positions? Section 3 examines the argument structure of the DP. With deverbal nouns, there are theta-roles such as Agent and Theme; possessives function in ways similar to Agents. In Section 4, we'll see the head N moving to other head positions, e.g. D. Section 5 is a conclusion.

1.   The D, DP, Num(ber), and NumP

In this section, we first consider what occupies the D head and then what is in the specifier of the DP. Abney (1987) was one of the first to argue at length that there exists a DP. We also add a Num(ber)P(hrase).

In Chapter 2, we distinguished between determiners (going with a noun) and pronouns (standing alone). Both of these use the DP; determiners are only part of the DP whereas pronouns represent the entire DP. The list of determiners is given in Table 2.5 of Chapter 2 and simple examples appear in (1) with their trees in (2). Most people argue that the D encodes definiteness, specificity, and so on. Even when there is no overt determiner, as in (1c), I will assume there is a null D expressing genericity.

(1)　a.　The monsters
　　　b.　A monster
　　　c.　Monsters

(2) a.

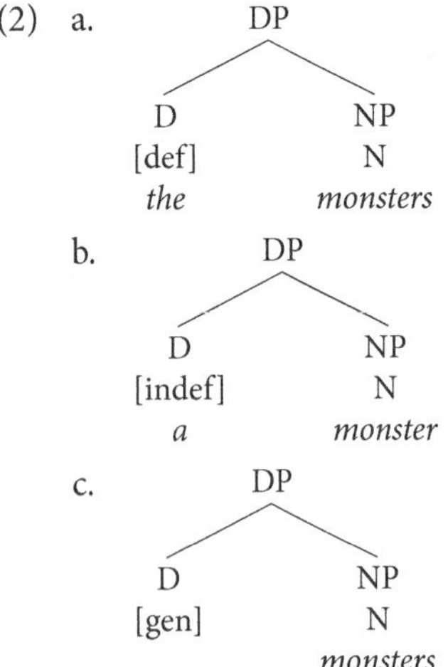

We can also have an entire DP, *that woman,* as the determiner of an N in (3), and the tree for that is given in (4). Because there are two separate DPs, I have numbered them as DP1 and DP2. A little later in the chapter, I'll argue that DP2 starts in a lower position.

(3)   That woman's nice car.

(4)

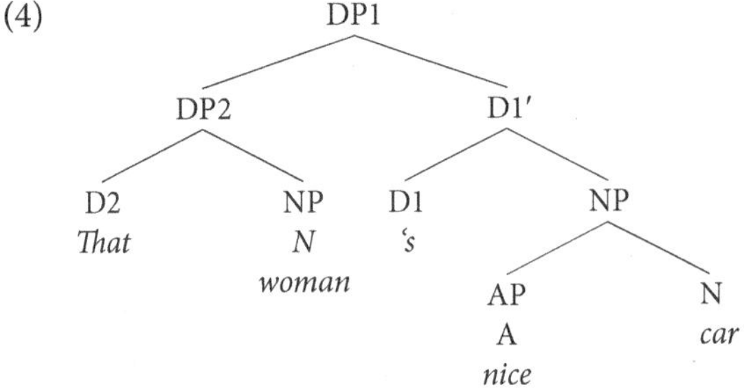

The DPs in (1) encode singular and plural number and therefore a Num(ber)P can be included, as (5) shows.

(5)

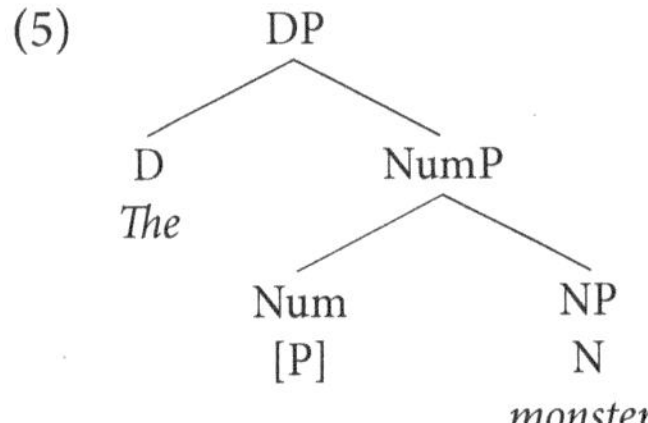

As we know from a previous chapter, the QP can be added to the DP, as in (6). Articles are placed in the head D but demonstrative and possessive pronouns are assumed (e.g. Giusti 1994) to occupy the specifier of DP, as in (6).

(6)

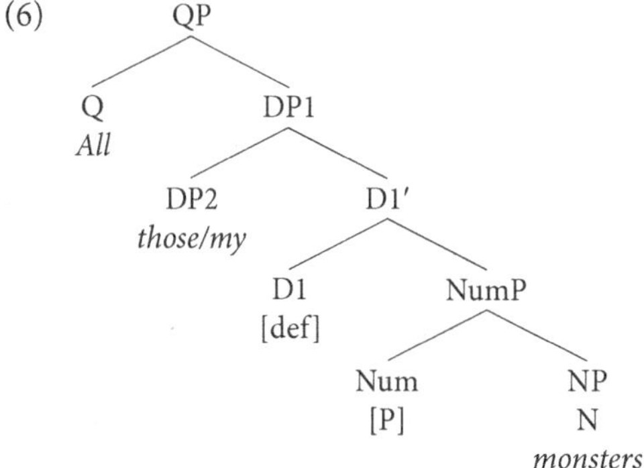

The demonstrative *those* in (6) is plural and may originate in the specifier of the NumP. I'll ignore that issue here.

Numerals can be argued to be heads in the Num head, as in (7a), and to move to D when a D is not present, as in (7b).

(7) a.

b.

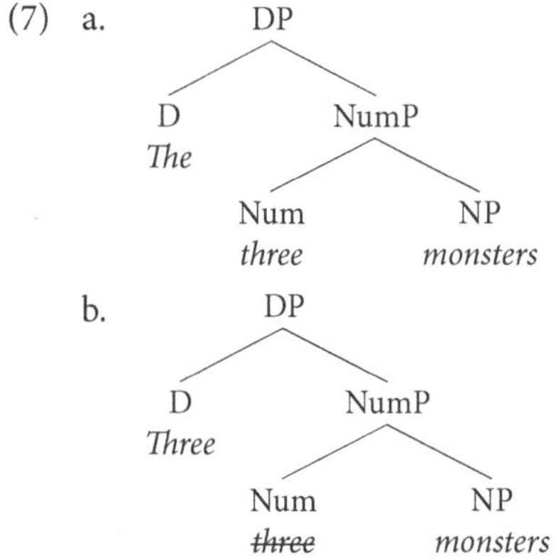

In Section 1, I have introduced a little more structure to the DP, the definiteness markers in D and number in Num. The next section adds adjective phrases.

2.   Adjectives

In Chapter 3, we've already seen DPs and NPs that include other lexical material. We made a distinction between modifiers, which are sisters to N′, and complements, which are sisters of the N. This is one approach to the placement of adjectives. In this section, we review that and discuss an additional approach to the placement of adjectives, resulting in two approaches, similar to what we saw with adverb(ial)s.

A typical example of the first approach appears as (8) where *tall* and *from outer space* are modifiers because they are sisters to N′ (and *chemistry* is a complement).

(8) a.

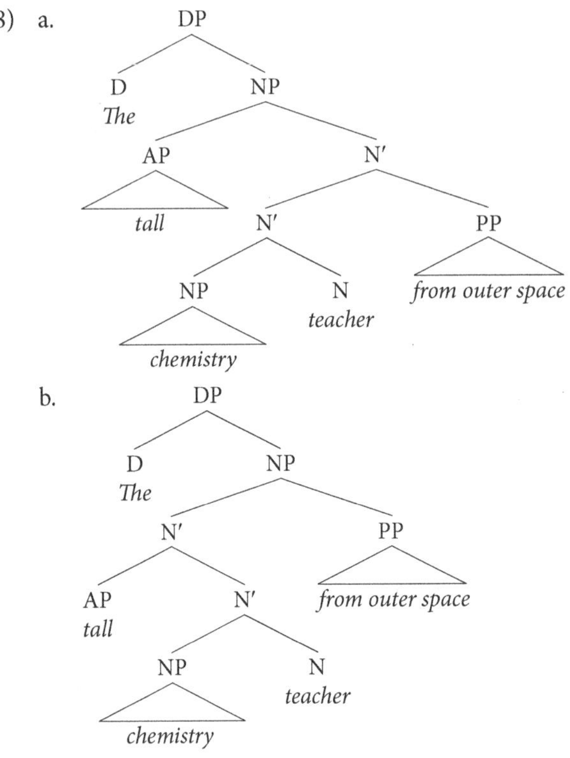

b.

In (8), there is no necessary order of the modifiers, as shown by the two possible (a) and (b) versions; the modifiers can be sister to any N′. In Chapter 3, I mentioned that a tree like (8a) was better. The reason is that the adjectives occur in the area between D and NP and occupy hierarchically ordered positions, as (9) shows. In the grammatical (9a), five adjectives appear in a certain order but, when the order is reversed in (9b), the result is odd-sounding. The order typical for English is that shown in (10).

(9) a.   The beautiful, large, fast, young, spotted leopard jumped out of nowhere.
     b. ˀThe spotted, fast, large leopard …

(10)   opinion   size   appearance speed age shape color origin material
       pretty, ugly large soft, sweet   fast   old round pink Israeli golden

(from van Gelderen 2010: 181)

One approach to such a hierarchical structure for adjectives is Scott's (2002), as adapted in (11).

(11)

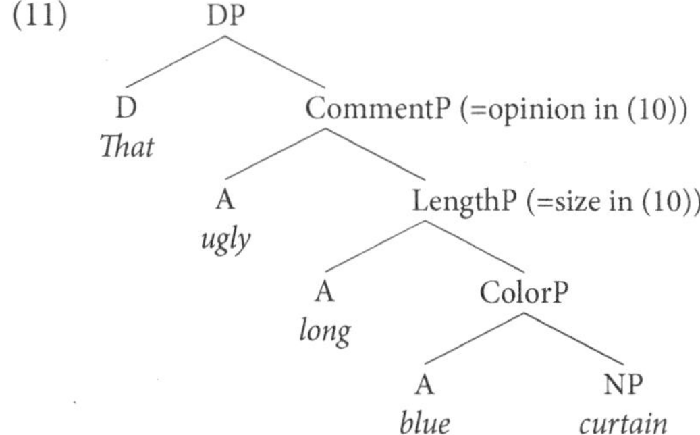

There are other classifications of adjectives, e.g. Cinque (2010). The question is how specific we should be!

In Section 2, I have provided two structures on how to fit in APs in the DP. As in the case of adverbs, one can do this by making the adjectives sisters to N′, as in (8), or by arguing for special hierarchically ordered positions, as in (11).

3.   Argument structure in the DP

Most nouns can have Possessors but not Agents and Themes. Such nouns include *car, table, shoes,* and *hand.* In this section, we turn to the nouns that have Agents and Themes; these are nouns that are based on verbs, e.g. *painting* in (12).

(12) Picasso's   **painting**   of musicians.
      Agent   Theme

In (12), *Picasso* is the Agent and *musicians* the Theme of the deverbal noun *painting.* As in the case of the VP, which we saw in Chapter 4, we'll assume that the Agent starts out inside the NP and then moves to the specifier of the DP, as shown in (13).

(13)

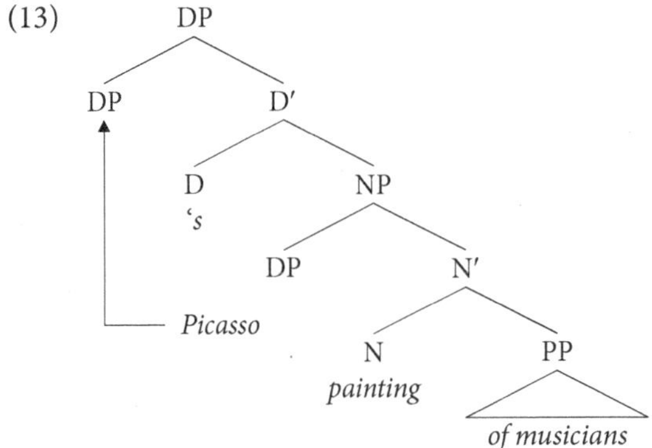

It is also possible that Picasso owned but didn't paint the painting, in which case the structure is as in (14). In this case, there is no Agent, just a Theme, and *Picasso* is the possessor. Because there cannot be both a Possesor and an Agent in prenominal position, I assume they are in the same position, namely the specifier of NP.

(14)

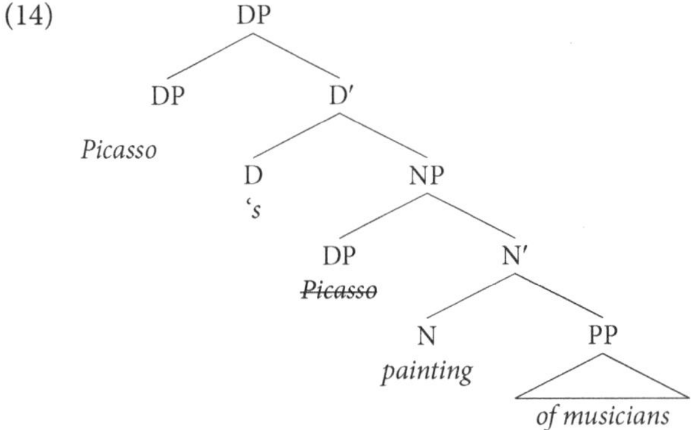

Other theta roles are also possible, e.g. *Amelia's gift of a dog to her son* includes a Goal as well as Agent and Theme.

In Section 3, we looked at DPs that are deverbal and where DPs and PPs inside it have specific roles to play, Possessor, Agents, Themes, and Goals, very similar to those in the VP of Chapter 4.

4.   N-movement

In Chapter 5, we came across V-movement. Inside the DP, there is also evidence that the N moves to a higher head position. Longobardi (1994) suggests this for Italian where articles occur before possessives (assumed to be in the specifier of NP), as in

(15a), with the tree in (15b), or where the noun moves to the D, as in (16a), with a tree as in (16b).

(15)   a.   *Il   mio Gianni*
           the my Gianni
           'My Gianni'
       b.

```
              DP
             /  \
           D      NP
           il    /  \
               AP     N
               mio    Gianni
```

(16)   a.   *Gianni mio*
           Gianni my
           'My Gianni.'
       b.

```
              DP
             /  \
           D      NP
           ↑     /  \
           |   AP     N
           |   mio    Gianni
           |___________|
```

The same movement has been argued for the cliticized article in the Scandinavian languages, as in (17a–b) from Swedish and the construct state nominal in Semitic, as in (18a–b) from Hebrew (for the latter, see Ritter 1991). The analysis given for the latter is that the possessor starts out in the specifier of the NP whose N moves to the D, as shown in (18b).

(17)   a.   *hus-et*
           house-DEF
           'the house.'
       b.

```
              DP
             /  \
           D      NP
          -et      N
           ↑______ hus
```

(18)   a.   *beyt   ha-iS*
           home   the-man
           'the man's home

b.

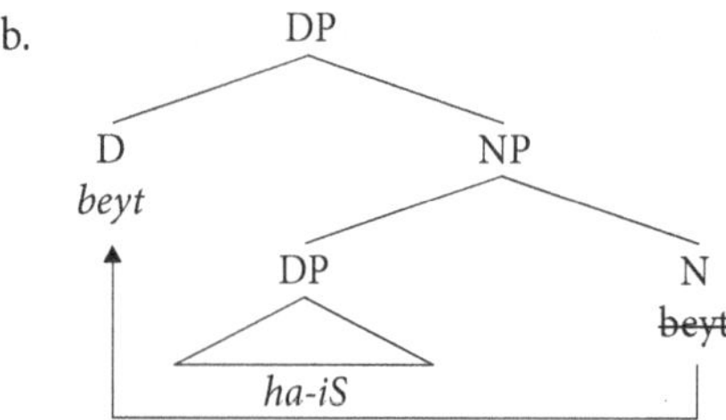

There are more complicated cases. For instance, Maori (19a) can have just the D, or a demonstrative, in (19b), or a movement of the article and noun to precede *nei*, as in (19c).

(19) a. ***te* *tangata***
DEF man,
'the man.'
   b. ***tenei* *tangata***
'this man.'
   c. ***te* *tangata* *nei***
DEF man   this
'this man.'   (Prytz Johansen 1948: 5–6)

One tree showing all three possibilities is given in (20). The minimum D is *te* to which the optional *nei* can move or not.

(20)

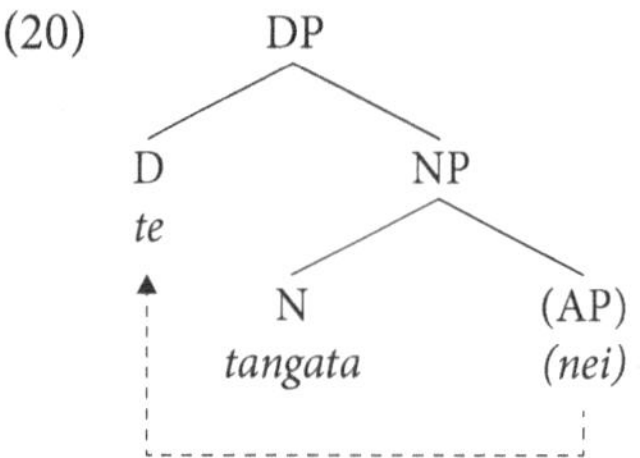

In this section, I have introduced N-movement inside the DP to the head D position. English shows little evidence and that's why examples from other languages are provided.

5. Conclusion

In this chapter, some background has been provided on the structure of the DP beyond a mere D head. Articles are heads and demonstrative and possessive pronouns are specifiers marking definiteness or the lack thereof inside the DP. A NumP marks the singular or plural number. Adjectives can be incorporated by adjunction, as in (8), or by occupying special phrases, as in (11). As in the case of VPs, the typical Agent appears more to the left than the Theme. Finally, nouns can also move in some languages.

After finishing this chapter, you should be able to draw a DP with a NumP, as in (5) and (7), and one with an AP, as in (8) or (11).

Exercises

A. Find a few interesting DPs in the below paragraph (from <https://en.wikipedia.org/wiki/Binge-watching>). No need for trees.

Binge-watching, also called binge-viewing or marathon-viewing, is the practice of watching television for a long time span, usually a single television show. In a survey conducted by Netflix in February 2014, 73% of people define binge-watching as "watching 4 or more episodes of the same TV show in one sitting." Binge-watching as an observed cultural phenomenon has become popular with the rise of online media services such as Netflix, N Play, Hulu, and Amazon Video with which the viewer can watch television shows and movies on-demand.

B. Draw trees for the DPs in (1) to (3). Leave out the NumP for now. Identify the theta-roles where present.

(1) My book.

(2) Rigobertha's sister's dogs.

(3) Their explanation of the disaster.

C. Why might you use a NumP in (1) to (3)?

D. Explain the difference between (8) and (11) in your own words and give some reasons why you might prefer one over the other.

More challenging

E. Figure 7.1 provides a DP that's difficult to parse but perfectly grammatical. Think about a tree that expresses this recursion.

Figure 7.1 The uncle of a … <http://www.gocomics.com/boondocks/2003/04/22>
The Boondocks, © Aaron McGruder. Dist. By ANDREWS MCMEEL SYNDICATION. Reprinted with permission. All rights reserved

F.   You may remember from (17) above that the definite article in Swedish is a suffix on the noun. This is also shown in (4a). How would you explain the lack of *-et* on the noun in (4b)? Drawing a tree might help.

(4)   a.   *universitet-et*   Swedish
            university-DEF,
            'the university.'
      b.   *Stockholm-s   universitet*
            Stockholm-GEN   university,
            'the university of Stockholm.'

Chapter 8

Features

Keywords: Phi-features, interpretable, uninterpretable, optional, intrinsic, feature parameter, feature economy, Affix-hop

Up to now, we have explored what constitutes the clausal backbone of the English sentence. In the present chapter, we return to the general framework and some areas, such as features and Affix-hop. Chapter 1 mentioned a considerable change in how generative linguists look at parameters currently, namely as choices the child makes about the features of the categories that it includes in its lexicon.

This chapter spells out which kinds of features there are and how a child knows so much about them. It also explains what interpretable and uninterpretable features are and how these are used in the Affix-hop that we encountered in Chapter 5.

The outline is as follows. In Section 1, I elaborate on the shift in generative grammar from Universal Grammar to more general principles that we saw in Chapter 1. Section 2 explains the notion of (un)interpretable features and spells out which features appear in an English sentence. Section 3 speculates about where features come from. Section 4 uses features in one specific instance, Affix-hop. Section 5 is a conclusion.

1.   From Universal Grammar to third factor

The Minimalist Program has shifted its emphasis from Universal Grammar to innate factors that are not specific to the language faculty. One of the reasons to deemphasize Universal Grammar is the evolutionary time it had to develop. If language arose in humans not so long ago, a very specific Universal Grammar would have not had the time to develop. The factors not specific to language are referred to as "third factors", which we saw in the third section of Chapter 1.

Generative grammar has also shifted its emphasis from syntactic parameters, such as the three outlined in Chapter 1, to ones relevant to the lexicon, i.e. features. The parameters are now, as (1).

(1)   All parameters of variation are attributable to differences in the features of particular items (e.g., the functional heads) in the lexicon.

In this model, the syntax of all languages is the same, consisting of merge. The differences emerge at spell-out because of the different features.

With the shift to features, the question can be asked what the features are, where they come from, how they are ordered hierarchically, and what their practical use is. These questions are addressed in the next sections.

2. Which are the relevant features?

Chomsky (1995: 230, 236, 277) recognizes semantic (e.g. abstract object), phonological (e.g. the sounds), and formal features. The formal ones are relevant to syntax and include categorial features, the case assigning features of the verb, and the person and gender features of the noun. The person, number, and gender features are usually referred to as phi-features.

Features are divided into interpretable and uninterpretable features. The interpretable ones are relevant for interpretation at the Conceptual Intentional (CI) Interface, such as the categorial and nominal person and number features. Unlike interpretable features, uninterpretable features are not relevant for the CI system and are transferred to the Sensory Motor system; they mainly involve the case features of nouns and the phi-features of verbs. Table 8.1 provides the uninterpretable and interpretable features of the noun *airplane* and the verb *build*.

Table 8.1 Uninterpretable and interpretable features of *airplane* and *build* (adapted from Chomsky 1995: 278)

	Airplane	*build*
uninterpretable:	[case]	[phi]
interpretable:	[nominal]	[verbal]
	[3 person]	[assign accusative]
	[non-human]	

Interpretable features have a value, e.g. first person singular [1S] phi-features but uninterpretable ones need to check with another element. So, T needs to check its uninterpretable person and number features (u-phi) with a DP whose noun has interpretable person and number features (i-3S, for instance). The noun itself has uninterpretable case which it values/checks with the T (or V). In Table 8.2, I provide a list of English features and their possible values.

Table 8.2 Grammatical Features in English, with their possible values

feature		value	feature	value
phi:	person	1, 2, 3	tense	present, past, future
	number	S, P	asp	progressive, perfect
case		NOM, ACC	mood	irrealis, realis

All languages have phi-features because they have pronouns, but not all languages have case or tense. Parameters account for where languages differ.

Let's review the checking of agreement and case in the TP (from Chapter 5) and add checking in the DP. The T has uninterpretable phi features in (2a) that it values through the interpretable features on the DP in (2b). The DP has uninterpretable case which it values through a finite T. In English, the DP then moves to the specifier of the TP.

(2)   a.

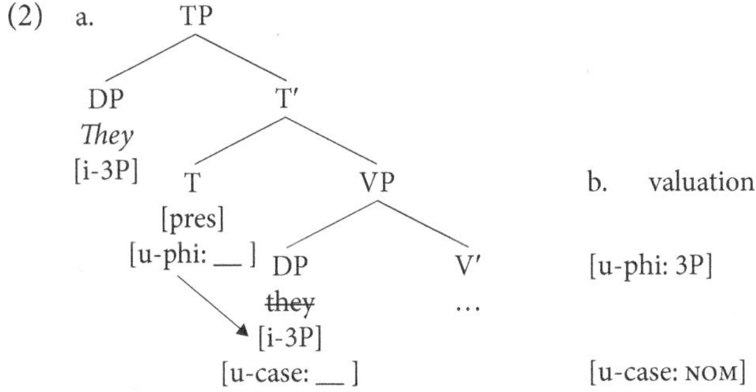

Inside the DP, there is also feature checking, as (3) shows for number. The phi-features on D check with the N head and get valued; the number features do the same.

(3)   a.

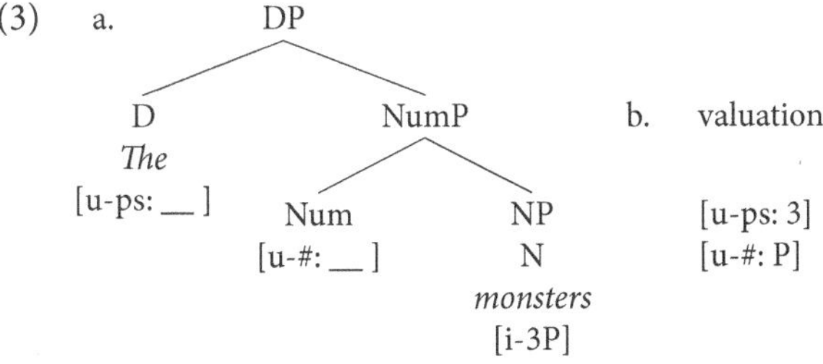

This section has outlined some of the grammatical features that are frequently used, e.g. person, number, and case features. It has also discussed uninterpretable and interpretable features.

3.   Where do features come from?

In this section, I ask how a child knows which features to use. I argue that some are innate and some triggered by these innate, semantic features.

Within generative grammar, the first linguists to stress a semantic representation are Katz and Fodor (1963). They emphasize the universal character of semantics and a connection to the human cognitive system. They use semantic markers such as [human], [young], and [male], to decompose the meaning of a word "into its atomic concepts" (1963: 186). Chomsky (1965: 142) writes that "semantic features (…) are presumably drawn from a universal 'alphabet' but little is known about this today and nothing has been said about it here" and, in Chomsky (1995: 24), there is the very cryptic statement that vocabulary acquisition shows poverty of the stimulus. That means Universal Grammar has to give some concepts, features, and structures for a child to acquire the words of its language.

When a child looks at the world, it knows how to categorize things; it is not just abstracting from its environment. This is clear with logical concepts, as the philosopher Geach (1957: 22–23) writes: "Abstractionists rarely attempt an abstractionist account of logical concepts, like those of *some, or*, and *not* (…). In the sensible world you will find no specimens of alternativeness and negativeness from which you could form by abstraction the concept of *or* or of *not*". Pinker (1984: 244–245) lists 50 semantic elements that could be universal and they include event, state, thing, count/mass, and substance/aggregate. Children start with words that have interpretable features and with nouns and verbs; grammatical words are rare, as is clear from Figure 8.1.

Figure 8.1 "Although"
Doonesbury, © G. B. Trudeau. Reprinted with permission of ANDREWS MCMEEL SYNDICATION. All rights reserved

Semantic features are, however, not the only ones and I will now look at the acquisition of grammatical features a little more. Here, I will assume a greater role for the third and second factor, as in e.g. Lebeaux (1988: 44) who argues that grammatical categories are centered in cognitive ones. Chomsky (1995: 230, 381) suggests that "formal features have semantic correlates and reflect semantic properties (accusative Case and transitivity, for example)". This means that, if a language has nouns with semantic phi-features, the learner will be able to hypothesize uninterpretable features on another functional head (and will be able to bundle them there). Initially, a child would use lexical categories (as well as demonstrative pronouns) with interpretable features (see Radford 2000) which then would be experimented with as uninterpretable features. A third factor principle, such as (4a), seems to be at work, with (4b) probably being part of the language-specific Universal Grammar.

> (4) Feature Economy
>   a. Utilize semantic features: use them as functional categories, i.e. as formal features.
>   b. If a specific feature appears more than once, one of these is interpretable and the others are uninterpretable.

Principle (4a) is adapted from Feature Economy as it appears in e.g. van Gelderen (2011) and (4b) follows from Muysken (2008: 46) who writes that "features which are doubly expressed (...) but receive a single interpretation, must be functional". Thus, innate concepts such as time, cause, agent, etc. together with the data available to the child (modality or past tense) trigger the grammaticalization of the semantic features into interpretable and uninterpretable grammatical ones. In Figure 8.2, some innate semantic categories are represented, as well as grammatical ones derived from them.

Innate	versus	triggered
shapes		classifiers
negative		negation
'if'		conditional
real-unreal		irrealis
mass-count		grammatical number
duration		progressive
causation		causative

Figure 8.2 Innate as opposed to triggered features

This section on where features come from is, of necessity, speculative. We'll now turn to a much more practical use of features.

4. Features and Affix-hop

This section will apply some of the knowledge we have about features and interpretable and uninterpretable features to a complex, practical problem, namely Affix-hop.

In Chapter 5, we saw that auxiliaries choose the morphological type of the verb on their right. In (5), the perfective *has* needs a past participle, as in (5a), not a present participle, as the ungrammatical (5b) shows.

(5) a. She has left.
b. *She has leaving.

Radford (2000) makes the argument that the features on the participle are the interpretable ones and I follow that. That means that, in (5), the uninterpretable aspect features of the functional head *have* check with the interpretable features on the participle *left*. Tree (6a) shows the unvalued state and (6b) the valued one. The participle ending on *left* is therefore responsible for the (present) perfect meaning.

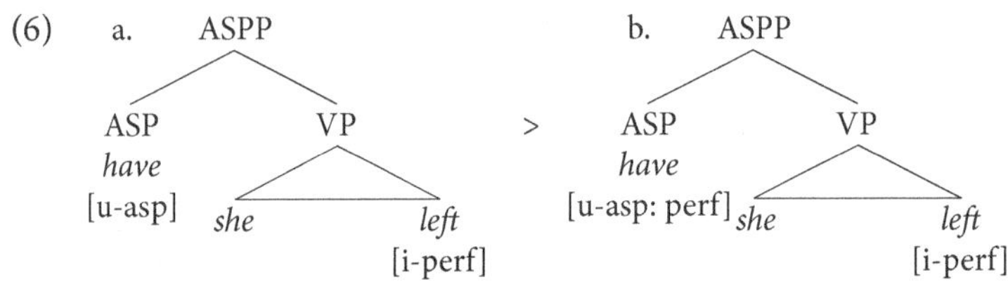

There are, of course, other features. Sentence (5a) is also present tense which *has* checks by moving to T as we've seen in Chapter 5. A tree that includes this is given in (7), again with values shown before and after valuation.

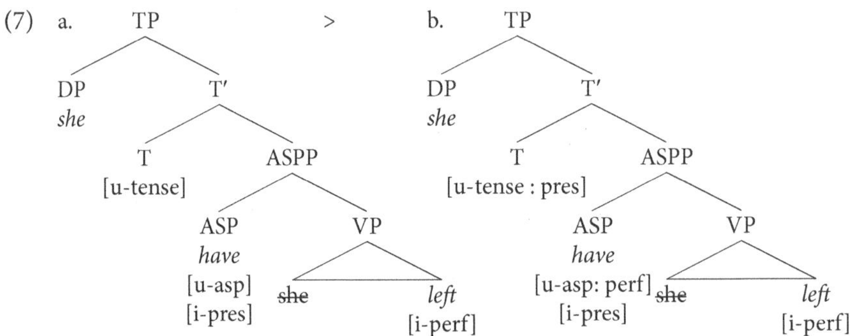

Another example of Affix-hop is given in (8), with a tree in (9) where the uninterpretable features are shown in a valued state. T(ense), M(ood), and ASP(ect) are shown but I have not shown the checking of T's phi-features and of the DP's case. The tree includes specifier positions for the MP and the ASPP but these could be left out. The relevant abbreviations in (9) are 'fut' for future, 'irr' for irrealis, and 'perf' for perfective. The infinitival form of *have* represents the interpretable irrealis features.

(8)   She may have left.

(9)

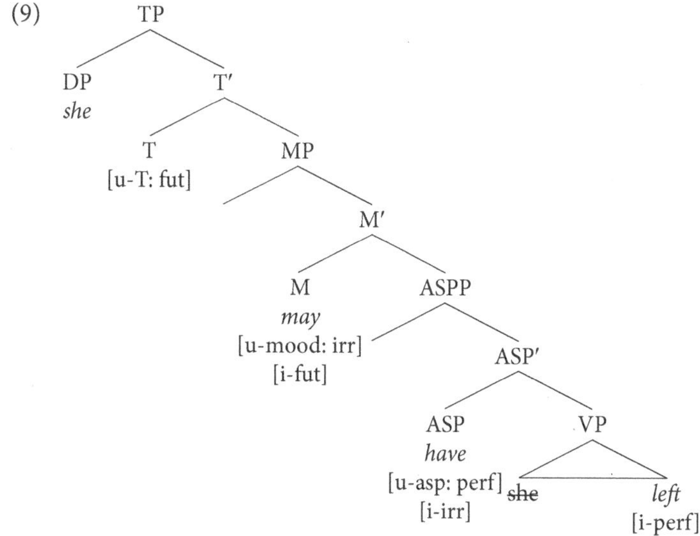

The model of checking, as in (9), takes words from the lexicon in a fully inflected way but with uninterpretable features that enable checking. It then checks them through the interpretable features on the auxiliaries and verbs.

The only features not yet provided are progressive and passive. For the latter, it is possible to suggest it is housed in the v, as is suggested in the Exercises to Chapter 5 and I will therefore leave it out of the discussion here. In (10), a structure with a progressive appears; the uninterpretable features are again represented as [u-] with their values added.

(10)

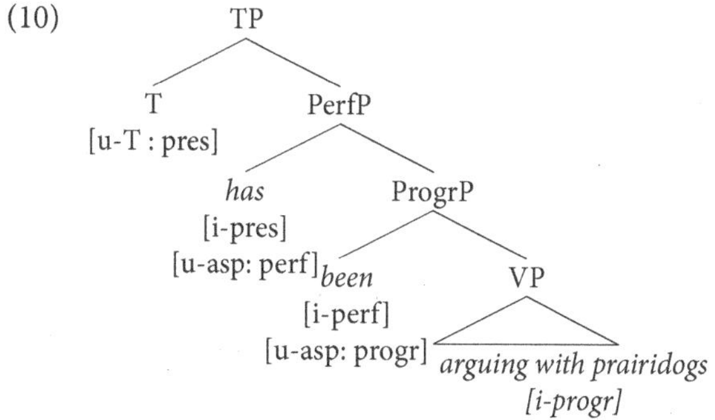

This section has provided an account for Affix-hop using uninterpretable features that check with the interpretable ones on a lower verb.

5.   Conclusion

In this chapter, we have looked at features in a little more detail: what are they and how do learners know which ones to include in the grammar they are building. We have discussed the more philosophical question as to how the language learner knows these as well as given a complex practical application.

After reading this chapter, you should have some sense as to the debates related to features. You should be able to draw a tree, as in (6), with some feature checking, and be able to explain Affix-hop in plain English.

Exercises

A.   Please provide some examples of grammatical features.

B.   In the text below (from <http://www.eastvalleytribune.com/columns/east_valley_voices/article_eb330f2e-cf57-11e4-937f-1b44fe6c2018.html>), find three uninterpretable features.

Have you ever considered how much you use the word "good" in your daily conversations? What does it really mean, anyway? Think about the last time someone asked you how your day was. What was your response? Did you happen to use the word good, by chance? Think about the last time you dropped off your kids at school. What were the last words you said to them as they left the car? Did you happen to say, "Have a good day." When I work with any group of students, the very first question I ask is, "How is everyone doing?" As you can probably guess, their answer is almost always one word – good. Even more, it's often said in a very monotone voice. It's safe to say that you've frequently used the word good, perhaps without even knowing it.

C.   More challenging
Draw trees for (1) and (2) putting as many features in as you can.

(1)   They were going to school.

(2)   It may likely be following the chaotic theory of fractal development   (COCA 1994)

D.   In Chapter 5, I mentioned that accusative case was checked by the object DP with the V or v. Could you put these features in a tree and show their valuation. You could use sentence (3).

(3)   I'll eat strawberries.

Chapter 9

Conclusion

Keywords: CP-TP-VP structure, formalist, functionalist, innate

This book has introduced generative grammar and provided the basics of a structural analysis of English clauses. In this concluding chapter, the main points of the book are summarized and some controversies are identified. I'll also discuss areas where readers have a choice to select a particular representation depending on what they are investigating.

The outline is as follows. The first section reviews the main points of the book and the second the debates and the choices readers might make when they write or think about syntax. This is followed in the third section by a review and a set of review questions.

1.   A Generative model and the clause structure

I'll start with a review of the framework, and then discuss the architecture of the clause.

As for the generative framework, it assumes that a child starts with innate semantic concepts and features to acquire its (I-)language. For a long time, many innate, syntactic mechanisms were attributed to Universal Grammar. We therefore started the discussion about Universal Grammar with a parameters' approach and showed how now more and more parameters are seen as lexical. Currently, the main innate mechanism of Universal Grammar is seen as merge, with its automatic hierarchical structures so relevant in, for instance, c-command relations. The framework is formalist, focusing on rules, and not functionalist, focusing on communication. Chomsky always stresses the primacy of thought over its external expression in language.

The basic spine of a clause consists of CP, TP, and VP. The VP is the layer that includes the verb with its aspectual information and the arguments with their thematic roles. The TP anchors the event to a time and therefore houses information on finiteness, tense, agreement, and nominative case. The CP connects the TP to pragmatic information (encoded in the mood) or to another clause. Each of these layers is expandable to incorporate one extra argument (for the VP), aspect and mood (for the TP), and CP-adverbials, mood, topic and focus (for the CP).

A derivation starts with a selection from the lexicon and then merges these elements, from bottom to top. In the current model (Chomsky 2015), the labeling (as DP, CP, etc.) is done as the structure is handed over to the semantic and phonological interfaces, i.e. the Conceptual Intentional and Sensory Motor, respectively. I have provided labels in the book, for convenience and because not everyone agrees that merge is without labels.

In a simple CP-TP-VP sentence, there can be XP-movement of topic, focus, and *wh*-elements and head-movement of the V and the T. There is of course also recursion/embedding of CPs within CPs. If one (or more) of the arguments is clausal, the question is what kind that CP is: ECM, Raising, Control, or full CP.

Other points we have discussed are c-command, empty categories (PRO, pro, copies), uninterpretable and interpretable features, and the internal structure of the DP.

2. Finding your own tree

Throughout this book, I have provided alternative analyses for certain phenomena. In this chapter, I summarize these options and a few other debates. Ultimately, it is up to you, the reader/user, to choose a particular analysis and to justify it.

Perhaps the most basic question is how 'bare' your tree can/should be. For instance, if there is no overt marker of mood in the main clause, do we need to add a CP as the topmost phrase? In the trees that I have drawn I have not indicated this top declarative CP, mainly to save space. In the case of DPs, I have added a null D to express that the DP is generic. In the case of copies, I have sometimes crossed out the phrase as well as the lexical element.

Another important question is whether modifiers have fixed or adjoined positions. We specifically saw that in Chapters 5 and 7. From an empirical point of view, there is no denying that adverbs and adjectives are hierarchically ordered vis à vis each other. Whether one makes sure of this order by means of a fixed structure or just position in the tree is an open question, in my mind.

I have portrayed the checking of affixes in Chapter 8 through an uninterpretable feature on a higher node with the interpretable feature of a lower node. Adger (2003) does it another way. I think my method works better for reasons I give more fully in van Gelderen (2016).

Inside the DP, there have to be number (and in some languages gender) features and their exact status is still under discussion. DPs are pretty variable across languages. The features that are needed, e.g. for agreement with the verb, also vary from language to language.

There are debates among linguists as to how to represent argument structure: is it cognitive structure (Jackendoff 2002; Pinker 1984, 1989) or syntax (Borer 2005a–b)? The way I have presented the argument is on the Jackendoff/Pinker side, with an emphasis on the aspectual nature of the verb.

3.   Review by chapter and review questions

Chapter 1 introduces the generative framework with its emphasis on the innate faculty of language in the acquisition process. Initially, parameters, such as headedness and pro-drop, were seen as part of Universal Grammar but currently only merge is. The parameters are now seen as operating in the lexicon. Review questions are:

a.   what is the headedness of English if you check all the categories, and
b.   what is the motivation to assume innate structures?

Chapter 2 provides basic information on the categories of English. It divides these in lexical and grammatical and argues that pronouns are a class on their own. Review questions would focus on the distinction between the categories, as in:

a.   how would you distinguish D and P from C, and
b.   what strategies would you use to find the adverbs and prepositions in a particular text.

Chapter 3 is a continuation of the basic information presented in Chapter 2. Here, we take the lexical and grammatical categories and show that they are heads of phrases. These phrases have a hierarchical structure that is important for determining the antecedent for reflexives and the negative necessary for negative polarity items. The chapter also discusses movement and the traditional notion of grammatical roles, such as subject, object, and adverbial. Review questions would involve:

a.   draw a tree for 'They will see an elephant in the garden', and
b.   why do we need c-command?

Chapter 4 argues that verbs come in three types, connected to durative, telic, or stative aspect. The arguments that accompany them are determined by the aspect; Agents with durative aspect, Themes with telic, and Experiencers with stative aspect. The chapter also shows that all arguments start in the VP (the VPISH) and that the VP can be split into a VP-shell to accommodate verbs with more than two arguments. It divides intransitive verbs into two classes and discusses the empty elements PRO and pro. Review questions are:

a. which are the theta-roles and aspect connected to the verbs *to write* and *to fall,* and

b. can you draw a tree, using the VPISH and the VP-shell, for 'The storm broke the ice apart'?

Chapter 5 explores the TP, arguing that it contains information on finiteness, tense, agreement, and case. The TP can be expanded to include grammatical aspect and mood. TP-adverbials are also accommodated in this layer and movement to and from T occurs. The NegP is also introduced. Review questions are:

a. explain in your own words what tense and grammatical aspect are, and

b. draw a tree for a sentence of your own choice including at least two auxiliaries.

Chapter 6 tackles what is included in the CP and the expanded CP. A CP indicates the basic mood of the sentence, e.g. indicative or interrogative, as well as the topic and focus positions and CP-adverbials. Evidence for *wh*-movement and 'islands' is given. Review questions could be:

a. provide examples of three CP-adverbials, and

b. how do we distinguish focus from topic in English?

Chapter 7 is about the DP which is not part of the clausal spine but which has its own spine with a DP and a NumP and an NP. The DP provides information on (in)definiteness, the NumP about number, and the NP about the arguments (if any) and the modifiers (adjectives). Questions are:

a. explain the ambiguity of 'a chocolate factory', and

b. provide a tree for one of the meanings.

Chapter 8 talks about the different kinds of features, e.g. phi, case, and tense, as well as about the nature of these features, interpretable or uninterpretable. It is more speculative in its discussion as to how children have access to these features but practical in the application of features to the phenomenon of Affix-hop. Questions could be:

a. name three grammatical features of English, and

b. explain uninterpretable features in your own words.

4.   Conclusion

This chapter has reviewed the most important parts of this book. Apart from an introduction to generative grammar, it should give the user a good grasp on the structure of a sentence and on how to draw a tree.

Review

A. Take one or two pages of your own writing, and identify if you use:

1. Raising, control, and ECM verbs
2. Reflexives and Negative Polarity Items
3. Coordination
4. Types of adverbials
5. Complex VPs, e.g. with adverbials, and complex DPs, e.g. *the chemistry teacher*
6. Expletive subjects and auxiliary verbs
7. Questions and floating quantifiers
8. Anything else?

You can finish this assignment by printing out the page with double or triple spacing and underlining or circling your constructions. Comment briefly on what strikes you about your own prose.

B. Then (try to) draw a tree for one of your more challenging sentences! In doing this, keep in mind the VPISH, the vP-shell, and the features.

Bibliography

Abney, Steven. 1987. The English Noun Phrase in its Sentential Aspect. PhD dissertation, MIT.

Adger, David. 2003. *Core Syntax*. Oxford: Oxford University Press.

Arnauld, Antoine & Nicole, Pierre. 1662[1965]. *La logique ou l'art de penser*. Paris: Presses Universitaires de France.

Baker, Mark. 2008. *The Syntax of Agreement and Concord*. Cambridge: Cambridge University Press. doi: 10.1017/CBO9780511619830

Bickerton, Derek. 1990. *Language and Species*. Chicago, IL: University of Chicago Press.

Borer, Hagit. 1984. *Parametric Syntax: Case Studies in Semitic and Romance*. Dordrecht: Foris. doi: 10.1515/9783110808506

Borer, Hagit. 2005a. In *Name Only. Structuring Sense*, Vol. I. Oxford: Oxford University Press. doi: 10.1093/acprof:oso/9780199263905.001.0001

Borer, Hagit. 2005b. *The Normal Course of Events. Structuring Sense*, Vol. II. Oxford: Oxford University Press. doi: 10.1093/acprof:oso/9780199263929.001.0001

Carnie, Andrew. 2011. *Syntax*. Malden, MA: Wiley Blackwell.

Chomsky, Noam. 1957. *Syntactic Structures*. The Hague: Mouton.

Chomsky, Noam. 1965. *Aspects of the Theory of Syntax*. Cambridge, MA: The MIT Press.

Chomsky, Noam. 1975. *Reflections on Language*. New York, NY: Fontana.

Chomsky, Noam. 1981. *Lectures on Government and Binding*. Dordrecht: Foris.

Chomsky, Noam. 1986. *Knowledge of Language*. New York, NY: Praeger.

Chomsky, Noam. 1995. *The Minimalist Program*. Cambridge, MA: The MIT Press.

Chomsky, Noam. 2004. Beyond explanatory adequacy. In *Structures and Beyond. The Cartography of Syntactic Structures*, Adriana Belletti (ed.), 104–131. Oxford: Oxford University Press.

Chomsky, Noam. 2005. Three factors in language design. *Linguistic Inquiry* 36(1): 1–22. doi: 10.1162/0024389052993655

Chomsky, Noam. 2007. Approaching UG from below. In *Interfaces + Recursion = Language*, Uli Sauerland & Hans-Martin Gärtner (eds), 1–29. Berlin: Mouton de Gruyter.

Chomsky, Noam. 2013. Problems of projection. *Lingua* 130: 33–49. doi: 10.1016/j.lingua.2012.12.003

Chomsky, Noam. 2015. Problems of projection: Extensions. In *Structures, Strategies, and Beyond* [Linguistik Aktuell/Linguistics Today 223], Elisa Di Domenico, Cornelia Hamann & Simona Matteini (eds), 3–16. Amsterdam: John Benjamins. doi: 10.1075/la.223.01cho

Cinque, Guglielmo. 1999. *Adverbs and Functional Heads*. Oxford: Oxford University Press.

Cinque, Guglielm.o 2010. *The Syntax of Adjectives*. Oxford: Oxford University Press. doi: 10.7551/mitpress/9780262014168.001.0001

Corpus of Contemporary American English (COCA), <http://corpus.byu.edu/coca>

Costa, João & Friedmann, Naama. 2012. Children acquire unaccusatives and A-movement very early. In *The Theta System: Argument Structure at the Interface*, Martin Everaert, Maria Marelj, & Tal Siloni (eds), 354–378. Oxford: Oxford University Press. doi: 10.1093/acprof:oso/9780199602513.003.0013

Dryer, Matthew S. 2013. Expression of pronominal subjects. In *The World Atlas of Language Structures Online*, Matthew S. Dryer & Martin Haspelmath (eds). Leipzig: Max Planck Institute for Evolutionary Anthropology. <http://wals.info/chapter/101>

Engdahl, Elisabet. 1983. Parasitic gaps. *Lingusitics and Philosophy* 6: 5–34. doi: 10.1007/BF00868088

Fillmore, Charles. 1970. The grammar of hitting and breaking. In *Readings in English Transformational Grammar*, Roderick A. Jacobs & Peter S. Rosenbaum (eds), 120–133. Waltham, MA: Ginn.

Geach, Peter. 1957. *Mental Acts*. London: Routledge, Kegan, and Paul.

van Gelderen, Elly. 2003. ASP(ect) in English modal complements. *Studia Linguistica* 57(1): 27–44. doi: 10.1111/1467-9582.00096

van Gelderen, Elly. 2010. *An Introduction to the Grammar of English, completely revised edition*. Amsterdam: John Benjamins doi: 10.1075/z.153

van Gelderen, Elly. 2011. *The Linguistic Cycle*. Oxford: Oxford University Press. doi: 10.1093/acprof:oso/9780199756056.001.0001

van Gelderen, Elly. 2013. *Clause Structure*. Cambridge: Cambridge University Press. doi: 10.1017/CBO9781139084628

van Gelderen, Elly. 2016. Features and Affix-hop. *Acta Linguistica Hungarica* 63(1): 1–22. doi: 10.1556/064.2016.63.1.1

Giusti, Giuliana. 1994. Heads and modifiers among determiners. In *Advances in Roumanian* [Linguistik Aktuell/Linguistics Today 10], Cinque & Giuliana Giusti (eds), 103–125. Amsterdam: John Benjamins.

Gruber, Jeffrey. 1965. Studies in Lexical relations. PhD dissertation, MIT.

Hale, Ken & Keyser, Samuel Jay. 2002. *Prolegomenon to a Theory of Argument Structure*. Cambridge, MA: The MIT Press.

Halle, Morris & Marantz, Alec. 1993. Distributed Morphology and the pieces of inflection. In *The View from Building 20. Essays in Linguistics in Honor of Sylvain Bromberger*, Kenneth Hale & Samual Jay Keyser (eds), 111–176. Cambridge, MA: The MIT Press.

Harley, Heidi. 2002. Possession and the double object construction. *Linguistic Variation Yearbook* 2: 29–68.

Hornstein, Norbert, Nunes, Jairo & Grohmann, Kleanthes. 2005. *Understanding Minimalism*. Cambridge: Cambridge University Press. doi: 10.1017/CBO9780511840678

Huang, Cheng-Teh James. 1982. Logical Relations in Chinese and the Theory of Grammar. PhD dissertation, MIT.

Jackendoff, Ray. 1972. *Semantic Interpretation in Generative Grammar*. Cambridge, MA: The MIT Press.

Jackendoff, Ray. 2002. *Foundations of Language*. Oxford: Oxford University Press. doi: 10.1093/acprof:oso/9780198270126.001.0001

Kalectaca, Milo. 1978. *Lessons in Hopi*. Tucson, AZ: University of Arizona Press.

Katz, Jerrold & Fodor, Jerry A. 1963. The structure of a semantic theory. *Language* 39(2): 170–210. doi: 10.2307/411200

Kayne, Richard. 1994. *The Antisymmetry of Syntax*. Cambridge, MA: The MIT Press.

Kayne, Richard. 2013. Why there are no directionality parameters. *Studies in Chinese Linguistics* 34(1): 3–37.

Koopman, Hilda & Sportiche, Dominique. 1991. The position of subjects. *Lingua* 85(2–3): 211–258. doi: 10.1016/0024-3841(91)90022-W

Larson, Richard. 1988. On the double object construction. *Linguistic Inquiry* 19: 335–391.

Lebeaux, David. 1988. Language Acquisition and the Form of the Grammar. PhD dissertation, University of Massachusetts.

Levin, Beth & Rappaport Hovav, Malka. 1995. *Unaccusativity*. Cambridge, MA: The MIT Press.

Longobardi, Guiseppe. 1994. Reference and proper names. *Linguistic Inquiry* 25(4): 609–665.

Muysken, Pieter. 2008. *Functional Categories*. Cambridge: Cambridge University Press. doi: 10.1017/CBO9780511755026

Palmer, F. R. 2001. *Mood and Modality*. Cambridge: Cambridge University Press. doi: 10.1017/CBO9781139167178

Perlmutter, David. 1978. Impersonal passives and the Unaccusative Hypothesis. *Proceedings from the 4th Regional Meeting of the Berkley Linguistic Society*, 157–189. doi: 10.3765/bls.v4i0.2198

Pinker, Steven. 1984. *Language Learnability and Language Development*. Cambridge, MA: Harvard University Press.

Pinker, Steven. 1989. *Learnability and Cognition: The Acquisition of Argument Structure*. Cambridge, MA: The MIT Press.

Prytz Johansen, J. 1948. *Character and Structure of the Action in Maori*. København: Munksgaard.

Pustejovsky, James. 1988. The geometry of events. In *Studies in Generative Approaches to Aspect*, Carol Tenny (ed.), 19–39. Cambridge, MA: The MIT Press.

Radford, Andrew. 2000. Children in search of perfection: Towards a minimalist model of acquisition. *Essex Research Reports in Linguistics* 34.

Radford, Andrew. 2009a. *Analysing English Sentences*. Cambridge: Cambridge University Press. doi: 10.1017/CBO9780511801617

Radford, Andrew. 2009b. *English Sentence Structure*. Cambridge: Cambridge University Press.

Reinhart, Tanya. 1976. The Syntactic Domain of Anaphora. PhD dissertation, MIT.

Ritter, Elizabeth. 1991. Two functional categories in noun phrases: Evidence from Modern Hebrew. In *Syntax & Semantics* 25, Susan Rothstein (ed.), 37–62. New York, NY: Academic Press.

Rizzi, Luigi. 1982. *Issues in Italian Linguistics*. Dordrecht: Foris. doi: 10.1515/9783110883718

Rizzi, Luigi. 1997. The fine structure of the Left Periphery. In *Elements of Grammar*, Liliane Haegeman (ed.), 281–337. Dordrecht: Kluwer. doi: 10.1007/978-94-011-5420-8_7

Rosen, Carol. 1984. The interface between semantic roles and initial grammatical relations. In *Studies in Relational Grammar* 2, David Perlmutter & Carol Rosen (eds), 38–77. Chicago, IL: Chicago University Press.

Ross, John. 1967. Constraints on Variables in Syntax. PhD dissertation, MIT.

Ryan, John. 2012. *The Genesis of Argument Structure: Observations of a Child's Early Speech Production in Spanish*. Saarbrücken: Lambert Academic Publications.

Scott, Gary-John. 2002. Stacked adjectival modification and the structure of nominal phrases. In *Functional Structure in IP and DP*, Guglielmo Cinque (ed.), 89–120. Oxford: Oxford University Press.

Slobodchikoff, Con. 2010. Alarm calls in birds and mammals. In *Encyclopedia of Animal Behavior 1*, Michael D. Breed & Janice Moore (eds), 40–43. Oxford: Academic Press. doi: 10.1016/B978-0-08-045337-8.00014-0

Snyder, William, Hyams, Nina & Crisma, Paola. 1995. Romance auxiliary selection with reflexive clitics: Evidence for early knowledge of unaccusativity. In *Proceedings of the Twenty-sixth Annual Child Language Research Forum*, Eve Clark (ed.), 127–136. Stanford, CA: CSLI.

Sorace, Antonella. 2000. Gradients in auxiliary selection with intransitive verbs. *Language* 76(4): 859–890. doi: 10.2307/417202

Sportiche, Dominique. 1988. A Theory of Floating Quantifiers and its corollaries for constituent structure. *Linguistic Inquiry* 19: 425–449.

Stowell, Tim. 1981. Origins of Phrase Structure. PhD dissertation, MIT.

Vendler, Zeno. 1967. Verbs and times. *Philosophical Review* 66: 143–60. doi: 10.2307/2182371

Verkuyl, Henk. 1972. *On the Compositional Nature of Aspects*. Dordrecht: Reidel.
doi: 10.1007/978-94-017-2478-4

Zaenen, Annie. 1988. Unaccusative verbs in Dutch and the syntax-semantics interface. Technical
Report SSL 123: 317–335.

Appendix

Answers to exercises

Chapter 1

First a comment: The parasitic gap in (3) was noticed in Engdahl (1983) and refers to a gap that is dependent on another gap. There isn't a particularly good theoretical explanation so I won't come back to it.

Answers

A. Of the three descriptive parameters, Lucy has probably set the 'move-*wh*' parameter, but not yet the 'pro-drop' one. We don't have evidence for headedness if we assume that the *wh*-object has moved to indicate a question.
B. The word order is OV, so head-final. A translation is hard because we don't know how Hopi marks definiteness, so it could be 'I saw the eagle' or 'I saw an eagle'. Kalectaca (1978) translates objects like these as definite. To determine the OV order, this information is not necessary, however.
C. In (3), the subject is a feminine speaker and that's why the participle *likhtii* is marked feminine (a masculine subject would cause it to appear as *likhtaa*). The subject is a nominative-marked first person pronoun. The lexical verb is also marked for present tense and the auxiliary for present tense and agrees in number and person with the first person subject. I have marked the variety as 20th century because currently a new progressive is necessary with durative verbs like *likhnaa*.
D. Hopi is pro-drop because, according to Kalectaca (1978: 24), it can leave subject pronouns out.
E. One aspect shown here is the creative, recursive, and unlimited use.
F. I found close to 80,000 instances of *myself* in COCA; one example is 'Making myself more aware of kids' needs … is important.' (Academic 2015). This sentence has a hidden antedent that is the PRO subject of *making*. In the BNC, I looked for *meself*, a non-standard form, and found 138, of which 'I frightened meself to death' (BNC conversation) is an example.

Chapter 2

A. Lexical verbs: *approved, put, hope, advance, provide, installed, breaking, provide,* and *said*. Prepositions: *with, on, as, of, through, by, on, on, of,* and *to*.

B. Complementizers/subordinating conjunctions: *that* (l. 2) and *which* (l. 5). Coordinators/coordinating conjunctions: various instances of *and*. Adverbs: *recently, just, recently, just, now,* and (*about*).

C. Checking a contemporary American corpus, I found that most speakers use *hard* as an adverb after the verb *look*.

D. Finite verbs: *approved, will, hope, will, installed, are, will,* and *said*.

E. Depending on the language you choose, it may be that there are few(er) determiners and pre/postpositions than in English.

Chapter 3

A. It is a VP; one can replace it by *do so* and move it to the left of the sentence. Note that *to* is a T and therefore outside of the VP.

B. When you read the first line you think that the speaker was wearing pajamas, but the second line makes that reading impossible and you have to rethink the sentence. Now, there are two interpretations left: (a) the elephant was wearing the pajamas of the speaker while being shot and (b) the elephant was shot inside the pajamas.

C. In (3a), the elephant is wearing the pajamas and, in (3b), the elephant is shot inside the pajamas or the speaker is wearing them.

D. The D of the DP in (4) is empty and, for reasons of space, I leave it out. *English* in (5) is ambiguous between being a student of English or student from England; my tree shows the latter meaning.

(4)

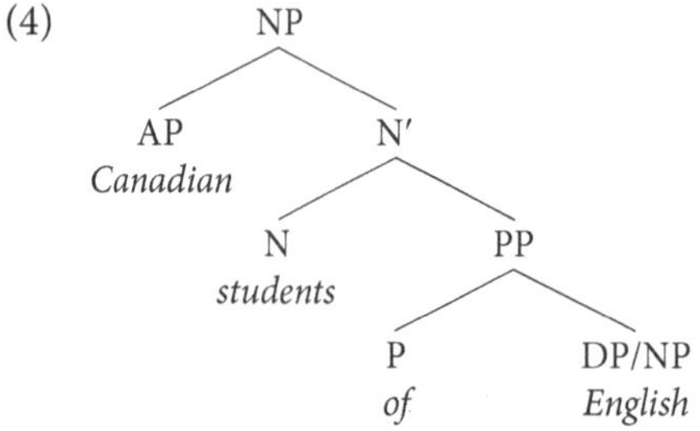

(5)

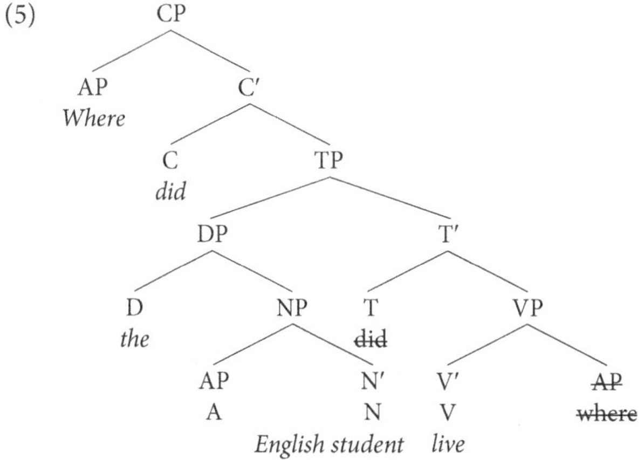

E. The negative *not* can be in many places but it will always c-command *any*. A tree with *not* as Chomsky-adjoined adverb is given in (6). In Chapter 5, we'll do a different tree, but *not* will still c-command the polarity item.

(6)

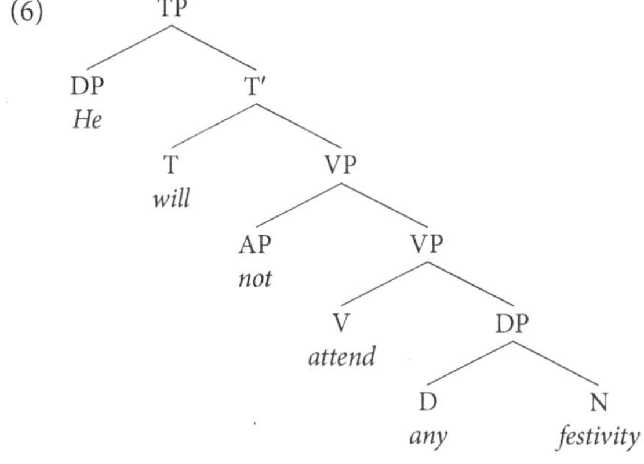

F. Adverbials in the easier text: *during the prolonged SW drought, right now*, and *decades into the future*.

Objects: *to have ... security, a sunny outlook on water security, a sprawling Sun Belt metropolis*, and *millions of newcomers*. It is possible to see *continues* as an auxiliary in which case *to have ...* is the main verb and not an object.

Adverbials in the harder text: *by forging ... alliances, to get ... books, to making ... bearable*, and *to earn ... appreciated*.

Objects: *its complex politics, their way, machiavellian alliances, candy, the tea, office life*, and *the respect of your colleagues*.

Chapter 4

A. An example of a transitive verb in German would be *essen* 'eat' and *schicken* 'send' would be of a ditransitive one.

B. Five unaccusatives are *arrive, appear, exist, depart,* and *fall*; five unergatives are *swim, walk, work, talk,* and *sleep*. When you search for *-er* endings to these verbs in e.g. COCA, you will find *arriver* and *exister* but only as a French verbs not an English noun. You will also find *faller* but as typos and as a last name. You will not find *appearer* or *departer*. This is all as expected because these verbs do not have Agents that appear as *-er*. This is very different with the unergatives that freely appear as *swimmer, walker, worker, talker,* and *sleeper* because they have an Agent not a Theme.

C. I have bolded the lexical verbs and bracketed the Themes. I have ignored copula verbs and sentences without verbs.
Palaeontologists **re-examined** [a 200-million-year-old fossil from Greenland], **re-igniting** [debate about the origins of mammals]. How old are you? What if, when someone **asked** you [this question], you **answered** [with the age of all humans]? [2.3 million years], you would **say**. What about all primates? Around 80 million years old. If you **wanted** [to **answer** for the whole of mammal-kind], you'd **find** [the answer **depends** [who you **ask**]]. In November a new paper **came out** that **stirred** [an ongoing debate among palaeontologists **working** [on the first mammals and their close relatives]]. Early-mammal expert Professor Zhe-Xi Luo, from the University of Chicago, **led** [a team **reanalysing** [the fossil of a mouse-sized creature **called** Haramiyavia clemenseni **using** [CT-scans]]]. They **found** [anatomical details that appear to **push** [this little beastie] out of the bushy crown of the mammalian tree, **relegating** [it] to the side branches]. This **has** [big implications for the age of all mammals].

D. The children are using unaccusatives as causatives, moving a verb like *go* from V to v. Certain unaccusatives cannot move in this way while others like *roll* can. This difference is something idiosyncratic that has to be learned about these verbs.

E. Both verbs are durative and their trees are given below.

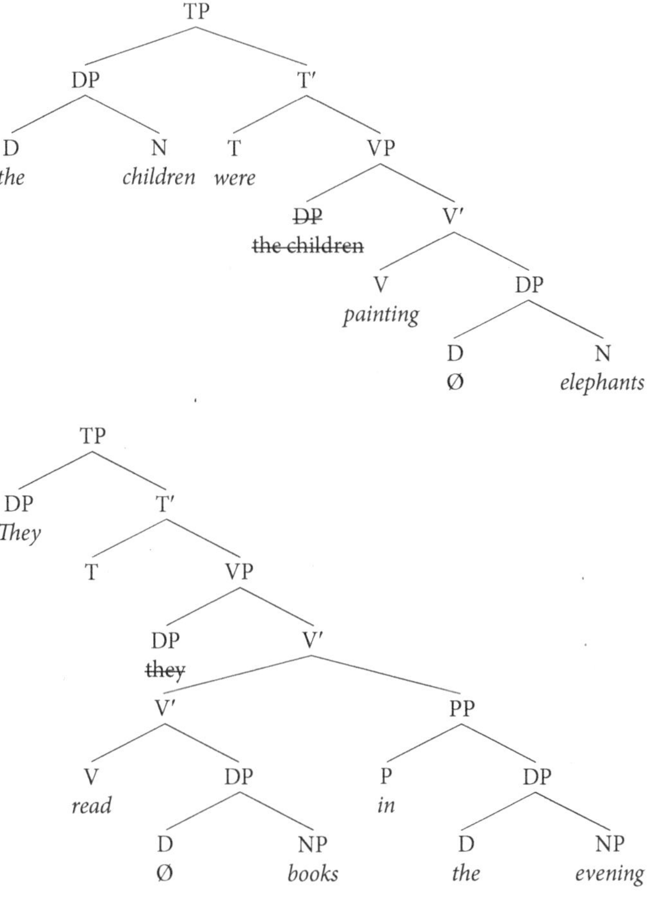

F.   (6) is an unaccusative, so I will just draw the VP but (7) needs a vP and VP. We could reverse the order of the V and DP too; nothing hinges on that.

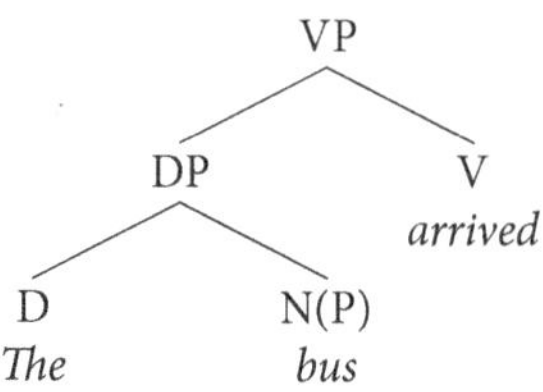

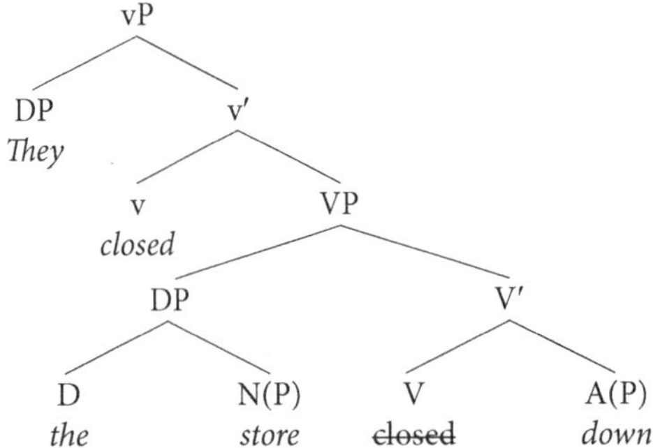

(8) is again unaccusative and (9) causative, so their trees are like (6) and (7), respectively, but given below. (10) is like (9).

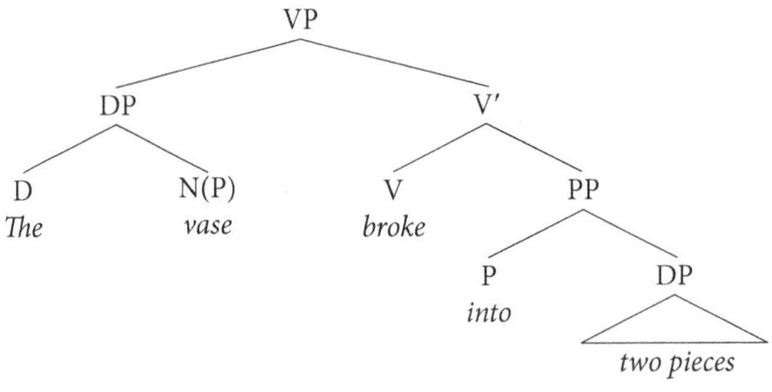

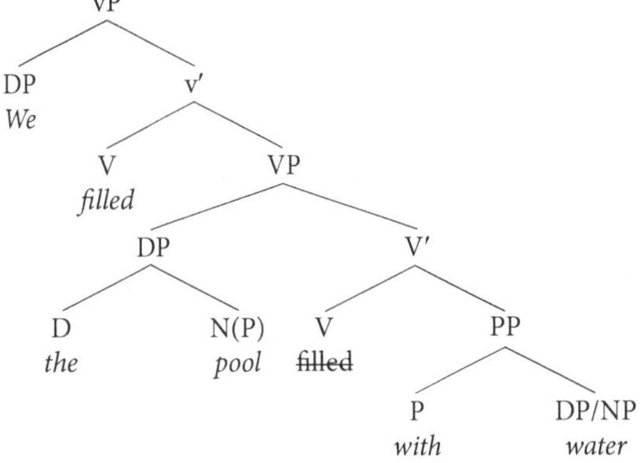

G. Examples:
I wanted PRO to visit Timbuktoo; PRO to be or PRO not to be is the question.

H. The adjective *cute* is here being used as a verb. Being cute will cause the person inside to come out.

I. I am only drawing the bottom part of the tree and I have not marked the numeral and classifier inside the DP.

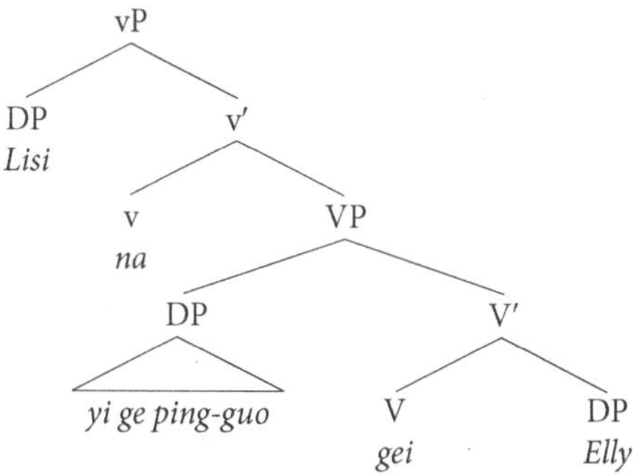

Chapter 5

A. A finite sentence is 'They have eaten'; a non-finite sentence is 'For them to eat'. The finite sentence has a nominative *they* and a plural, inflected verb *have*; the non-finite has an accusative subject *them* and a non-finite verb.

B. is (A, progressive), to (M, infinitive), is (A, progressive), will (M, modal), be (A, progressive), to (M, infinitive) two times, 're (A, progressive).

C. The subject *she* has nominative case and the finite auxiliary *was* shows agreement with this subject.

D. (2)

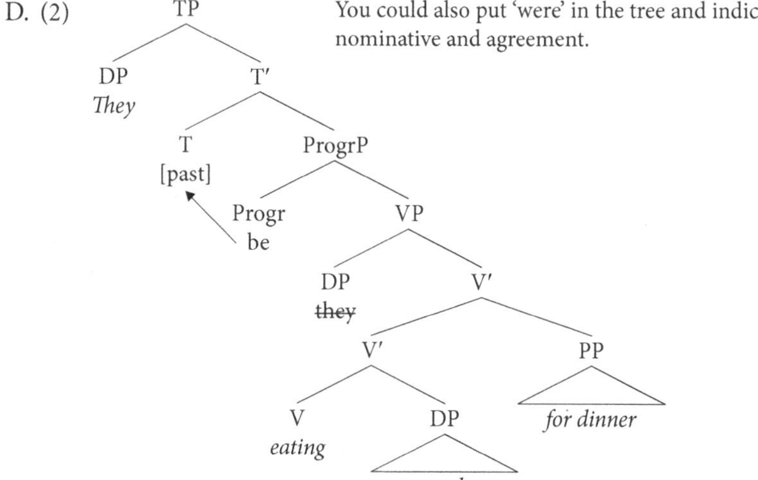

You could also put 'were' in the tree and indicate nominative and agreement.

(3)

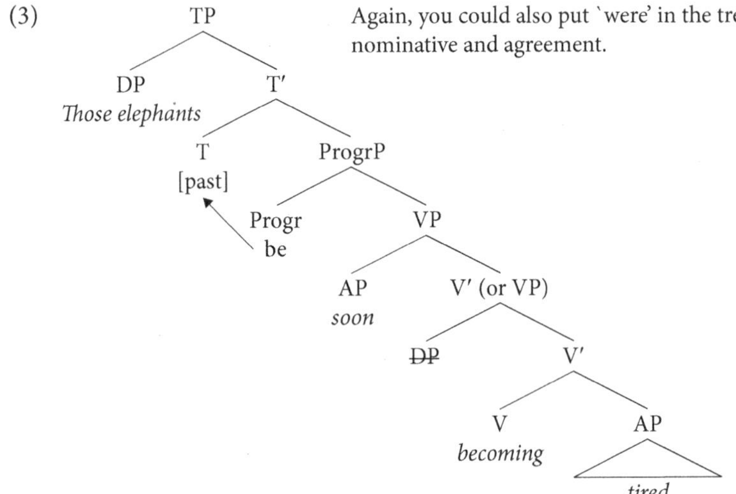

Again, you could also put 'were' in the tree and indicate nominative and agreement.

E.   A tree for the adverbs in (4), using designated positions, is given here.

(4)

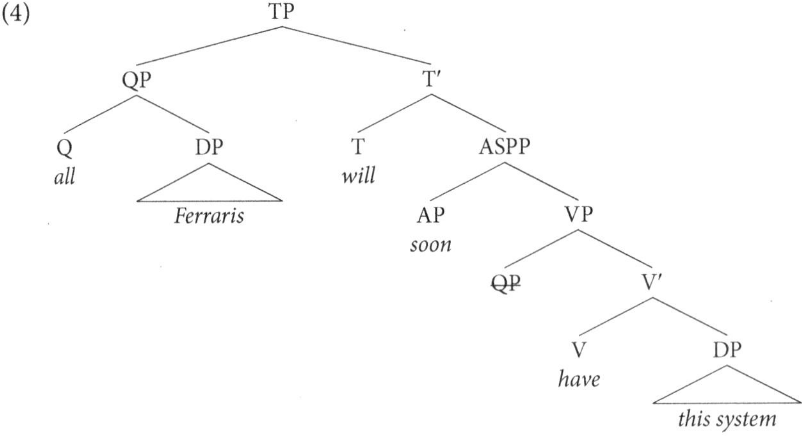

Trees for (5) and (6) are as follows.

(5)

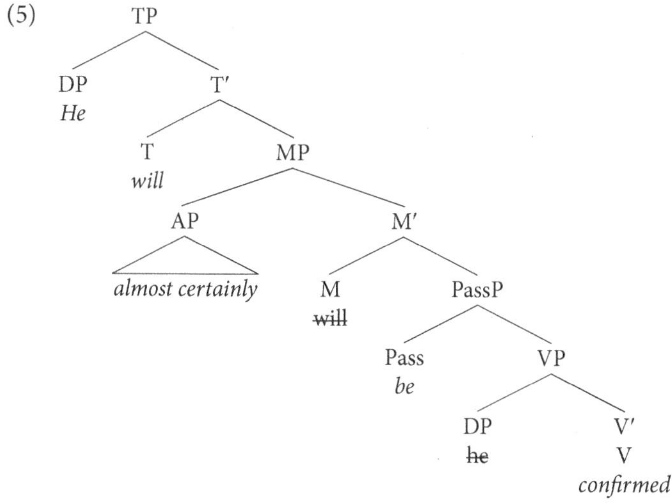

(6)

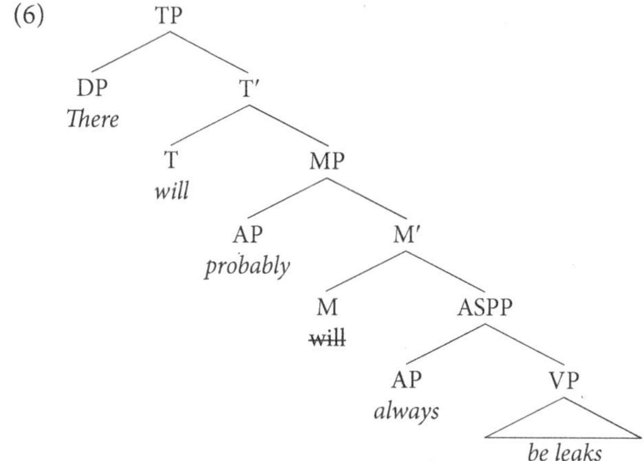

F.   A negative sentence could be 'We won't go there'. In the tree, I have used the VPISH and just the future features. There are two possibilities for *won't*: either *will* and *n't* will be adjusted into *won't* or *won't* is listed in the lexicon with negative and future features.

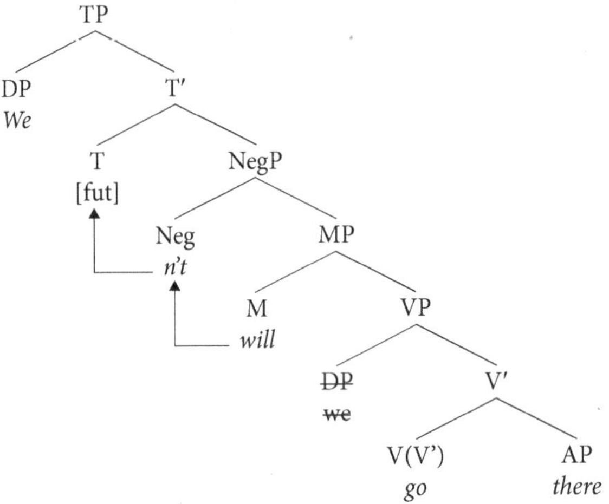

G. The finite verb precedes the aspectual adverb and has therefore moved to T. A tree with an adjoined adverb appears in (7a) and with a designated place for the adverb in (7b).

(7) a.

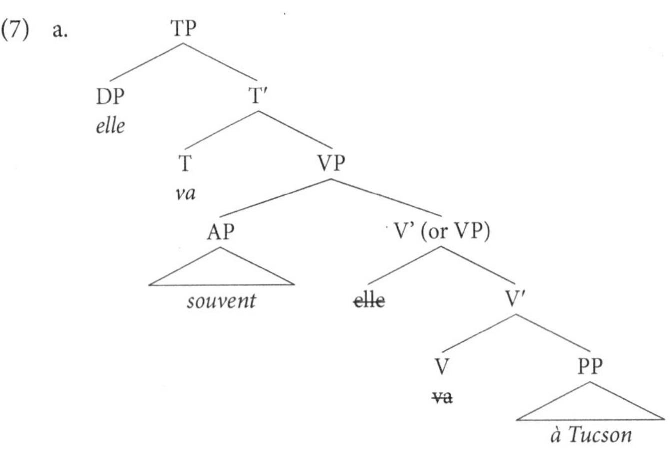

b.

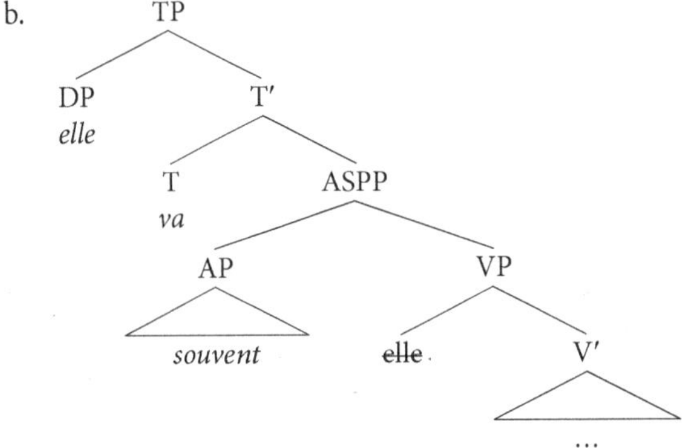

H. In (8), the aspect marker 'le' comes after the verb. You could think of the V as moving to the ASP, as in (8).

(8)

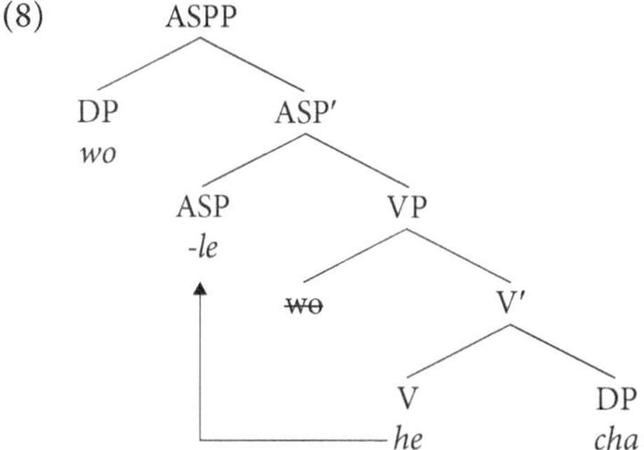

I. In (9), the speaker is making the past participle into a simple past probably because the verb is irregular. In (10), the infinitival form is used rather than the past participle form. In (11), *wanna* is used as auxiliary.

J. (12)   If we added *widely*, it could adjoin to vP or VP, as in:

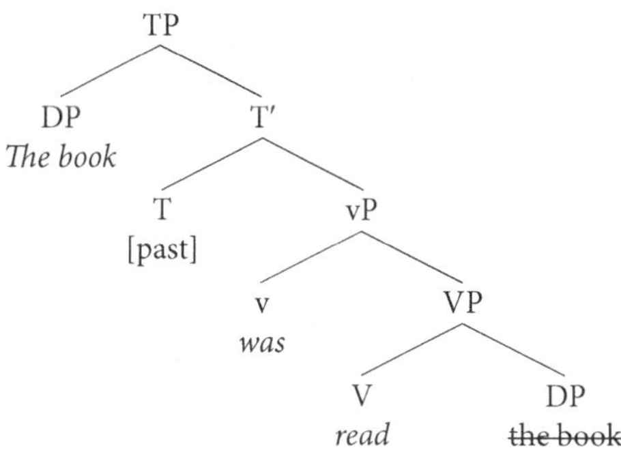

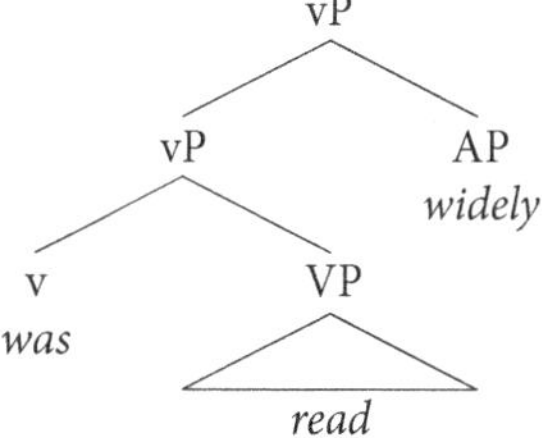

Chapter 6

A. The complementizers are underlined and brackets appear around the embedded clauses.

A Canada-bound airliner was forced [to make an emergency landing [after severe turbulence injured 21 passengers, including three children]]. The Air Canada flight from Shanghai to Toronto was diverted to Calgary [after the turbulence hit]. Eight passengers suffered neck and back injuries and 13 more were taken to hospital for observation. [The injured were in a stable condition], an emergency services spokesman said. Bing Feng, a passenger, described [hearing "lots of screaming" [as the plane became "like a rollercoaster"]]. Even enthusiastic fliers can get nervous [when there is some chunky turbulence around]. But [although people can get hurt [if they aren't strapped in]], turbulence doesn't crash airplanes. Lots of things can cause turbulence, but pilots can often predict [when it's coming], so they can either avoid it or put on the fasten seat-belt signs. And aircraft are built to withstand even the worst excesses of mother nature. Wings are bent [until they snap], hulls are tested by [attacking them with artificial lightning strikes]. In the most extreme examples, turbulence could potentially damage an aircraft, but it won't knock it out of the sky.

B. In (1), I have indicated the position of the subject according to the VPISH but have not used the vP-shell.

(1)

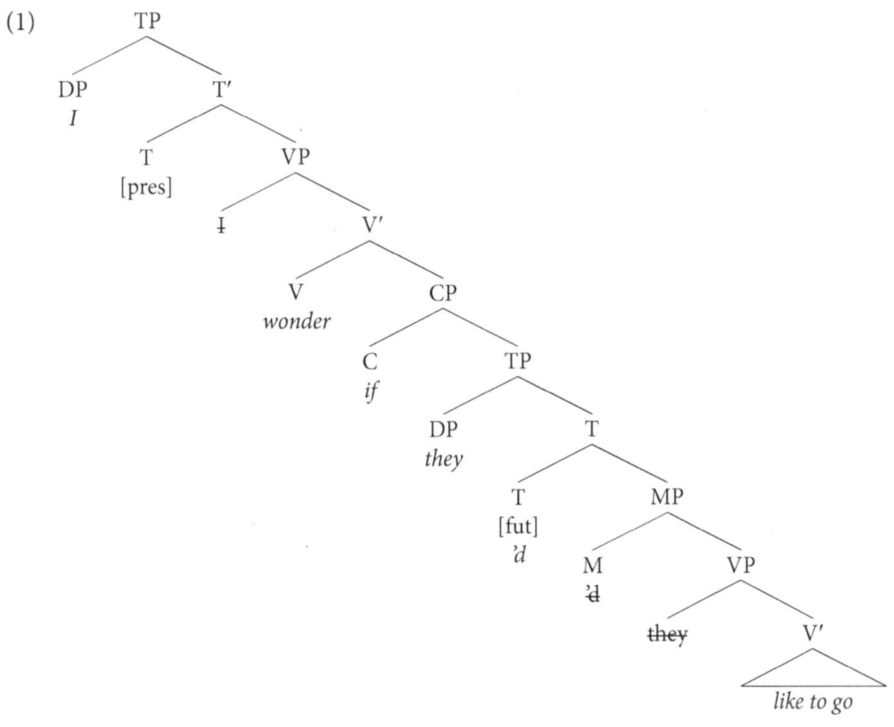

(2)

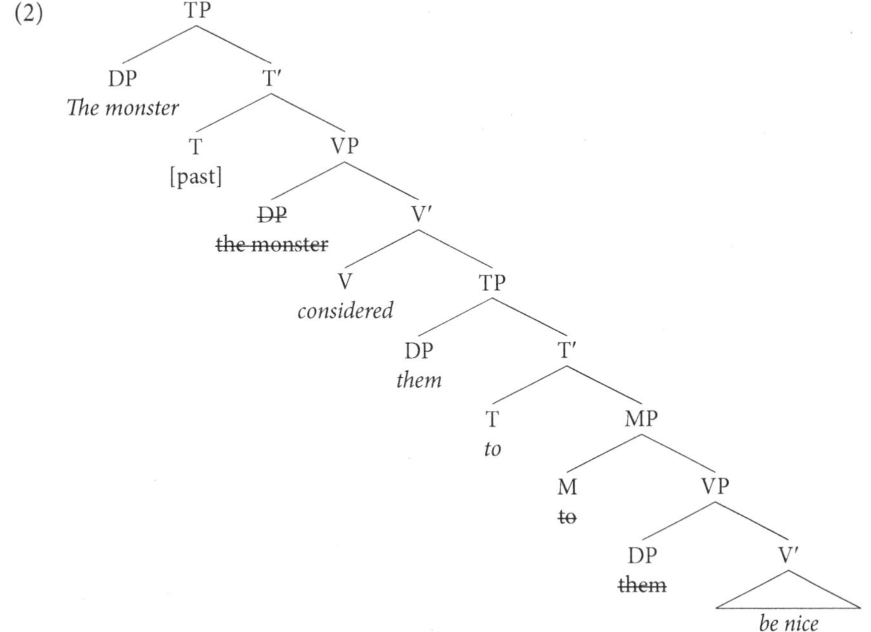

C. Children may use an auxiliary as a question marker in (3) and don't delete the lower copy in (4).

D. In 'Who did he say she talked with', the *wh*-element has moved from the object of the preposition of the embedded clause. A tree would be as follows.

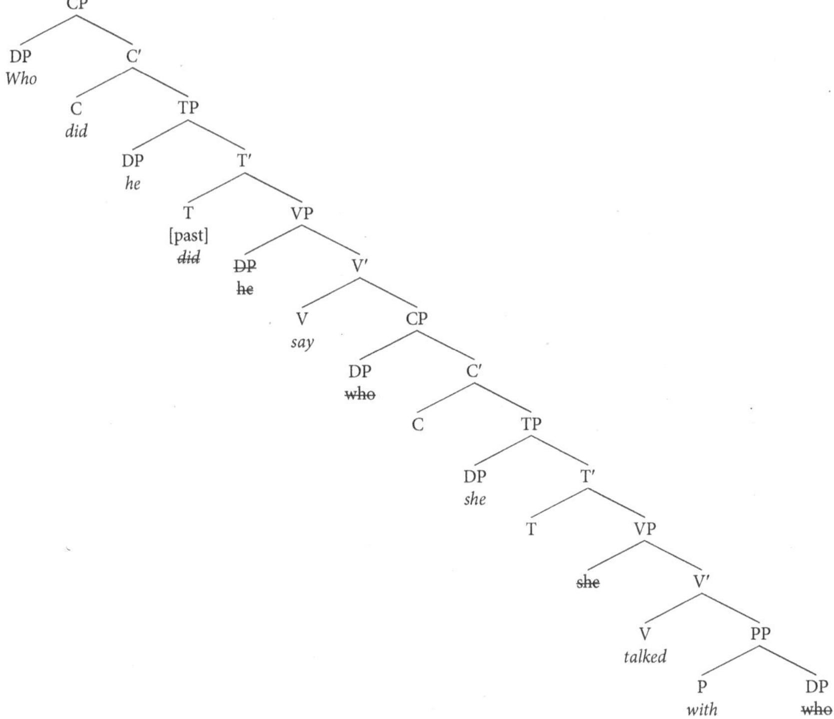

In (6), the 'he' has raised from the lower to the higher subject position.

E. Some languages need not move the *wh*-element, e.g. the example given in Chapter 1.

F. A simple tree for (7) is given below.

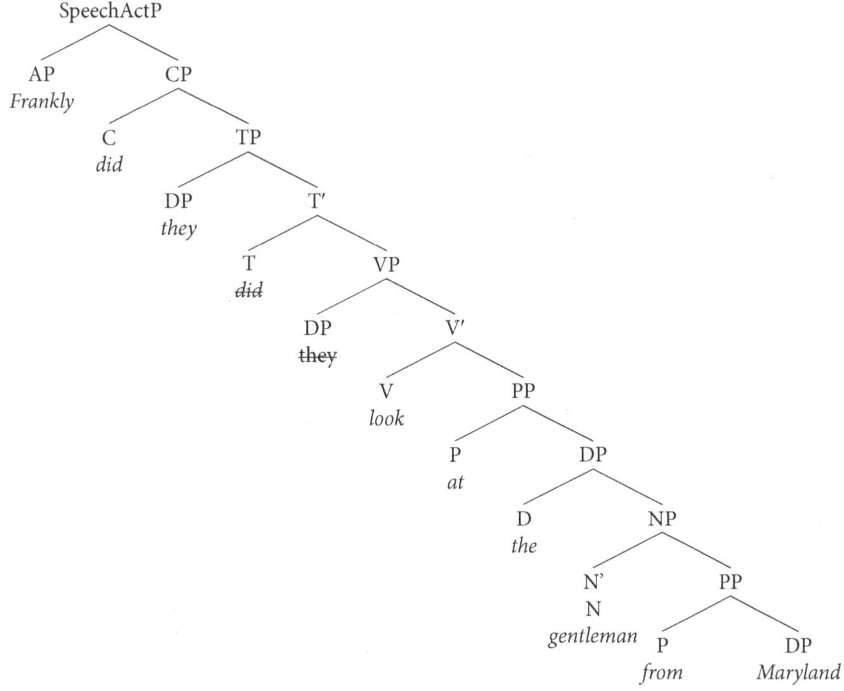

G. *Manage* in (8) is control, *plan* in (9) is control, *tend* in (10) is raising, *intend* in (11) is control, *threaten* in (12) is raising, *come* in (13) is raising, *happen* in (14) is raising, and *hope* in (15) is control.

Chapter 7

A. I have underlined a few of the more complex DPs:
Binge-watching, also called binge-viewing or marathon-viewing, is <u>the practice of watching television for a long time span, usually a single television show</u>. In <u>a survey conducted by Netflix in February 2014</u>, <u>73% of people</u> define binge-watching as "<u>watching 4 or more episodes of the same TV show in one sitting</u>." Binge-watching as <u>an observed cultural phenomenon</u> has become popular with <u>the rise of online media services such as Netflix, N Play, Hulu, and Amazon Video with which the viewer can watch television shows and movies on-demand</u>.

B. (1)

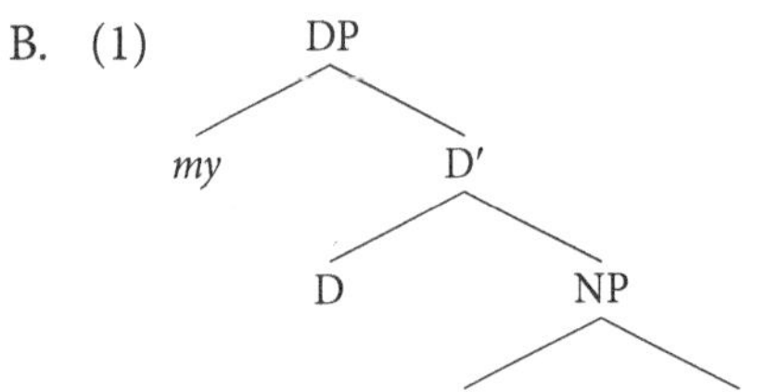

(2)

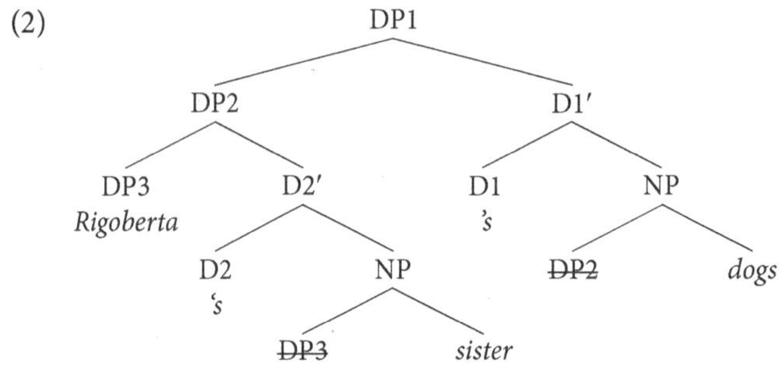

(3)

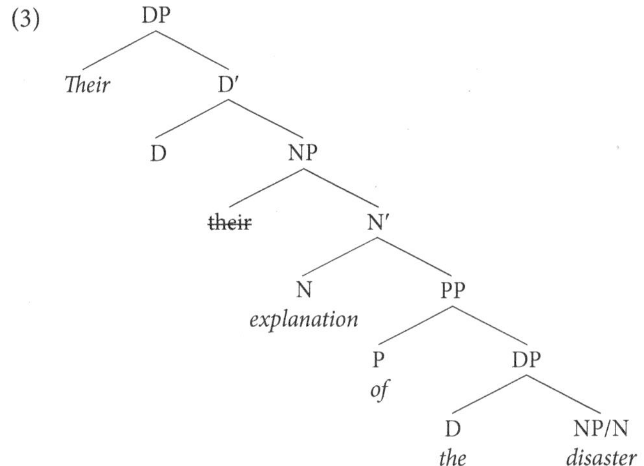

The theta-roles in (1) and (2) are Possessor and in (3) Agent and Theme.

C. The trees in (2) and (3) are relatively complex already and number isn't relevant. Adding a NumP to (1) results in (4).

(4)

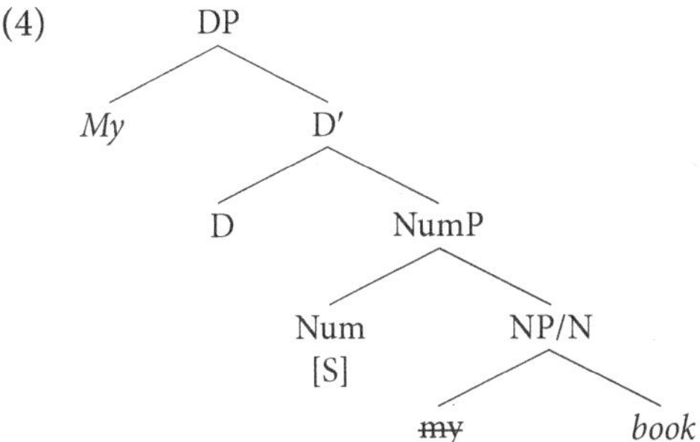

D. Adjectives can be accommodated by adjunction to any N′, as in (8) of the chapter. This results in free ordering which adjectives sometimes show. Tree (11) puts each adjective in a specially designated position. This explains their frequently strict order.

E. The basic tree is like (2) in question B, and goes somewhat like (5). To finish it, keep working on DP4.

(4)

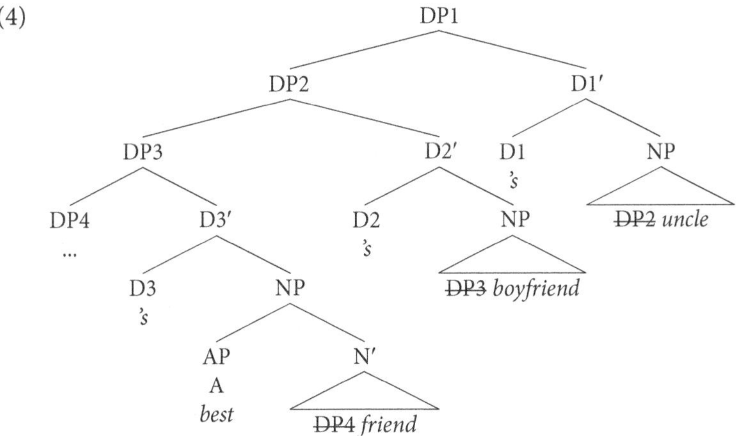

F. If -*s* is in D, a D -*et* is not needed. A tree might be the following.

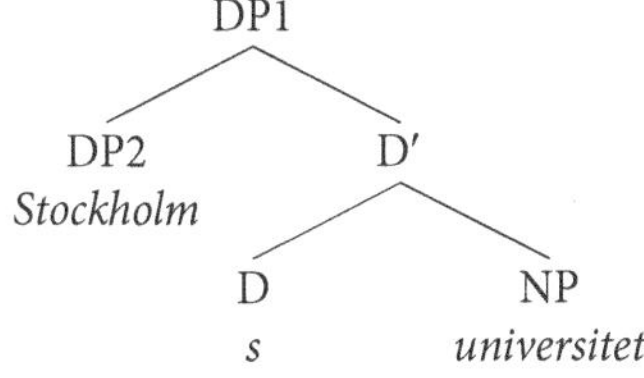

Chapter 8

A. present, past, 1, S.

B. I have shown all features: Have (u-asp, i-pres), considered (i-Perf), does (u-phi, i-pres), asked (i-past), is (u-asp, i-pres), doing (i-progr), can (u-mood, i-fut).

C. (1) a.
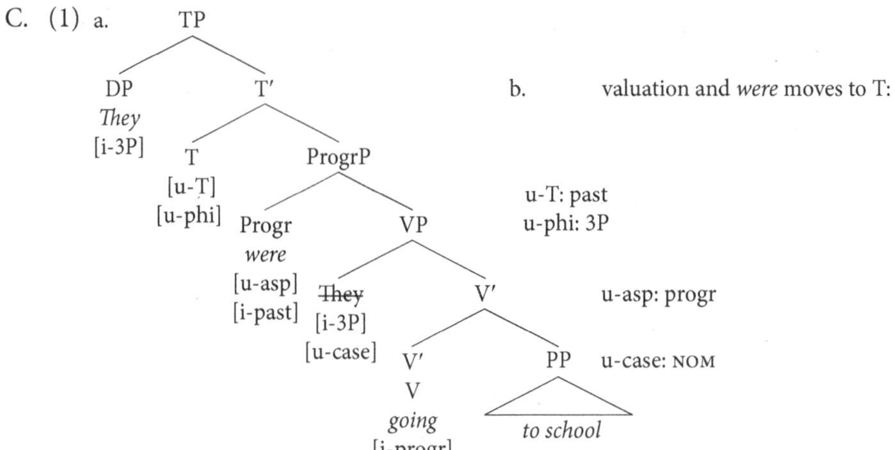

(2) a.
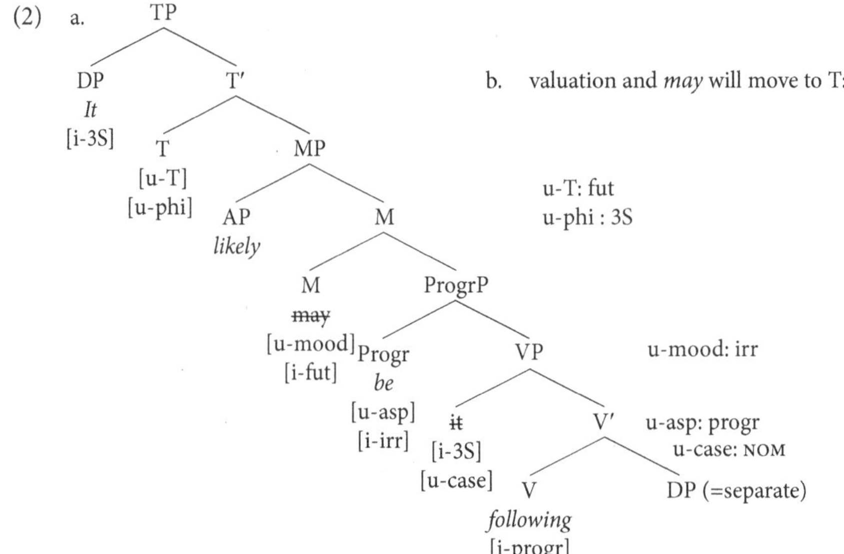

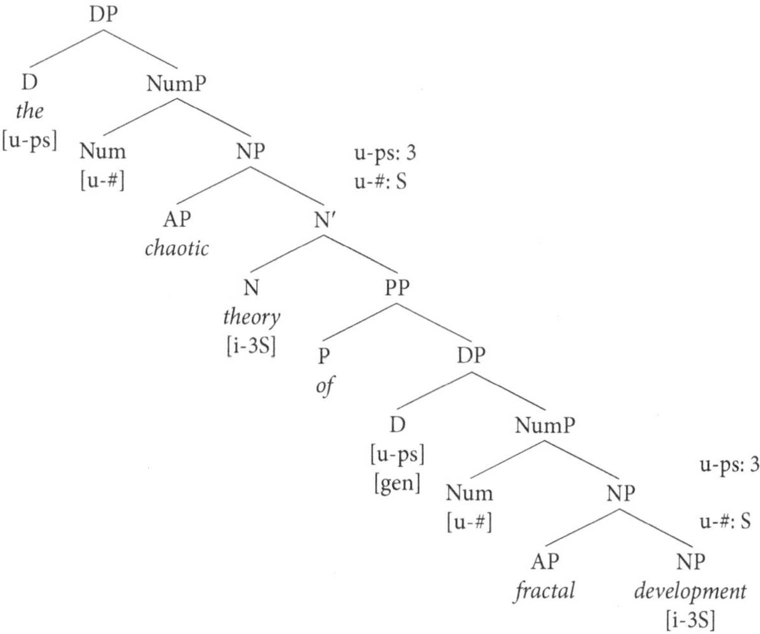

D. The auxiliary move to T and the valuation goes like:

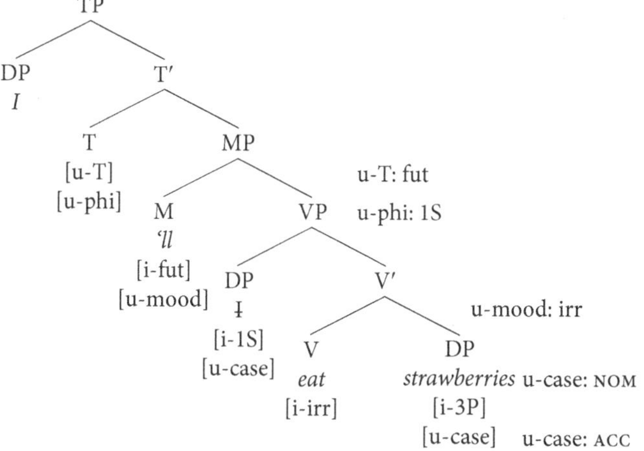

Chapter 9

Suggested answers to the review questions

Chapter 1: (a) English is head-initial (except for the N which has the Adj preceding it) and (b) children don't imitate (e.g. they use *drawed* rather than *drew*) and acquire languages easily.

Chapter 2: (a) The D and P introduce a nominal whereas the C introduces a clausal element. (b) Adverbs modify verbs while Ps precede nouns.

Chapter 3: (b) It explains the interpretation of anaphors, negative polarity items, and the hierarchical structure and (a)'s tree is here:

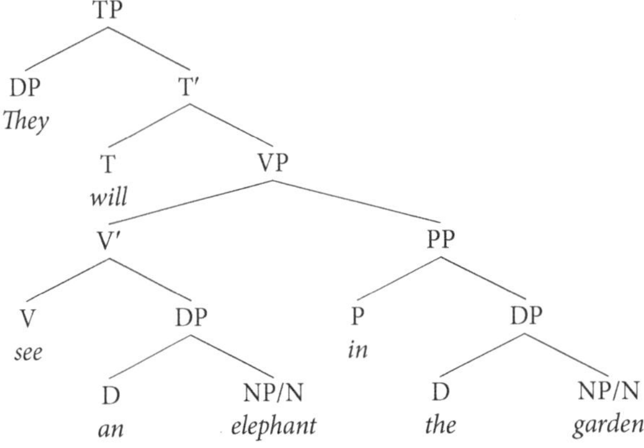

Chapter 4: (a) The durative verb *write* has an Agent and Theme and the telic verb *fall* just a Theme and tree for (b) is here:

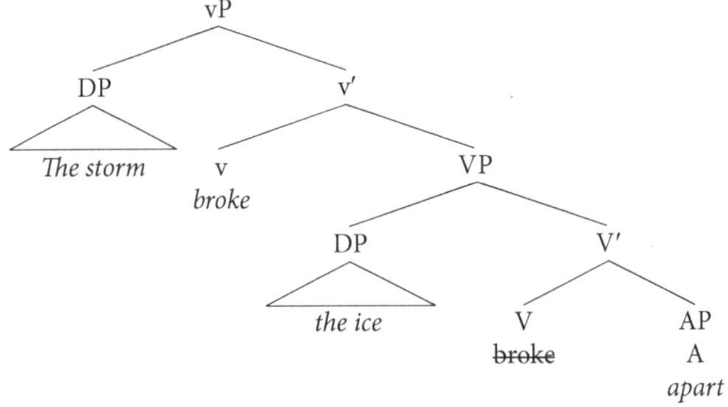

Chapter 5: (a) Tense is about points in time that the event can be anchored to; grammatical aspect is about the manner the event happened and (b) could be:

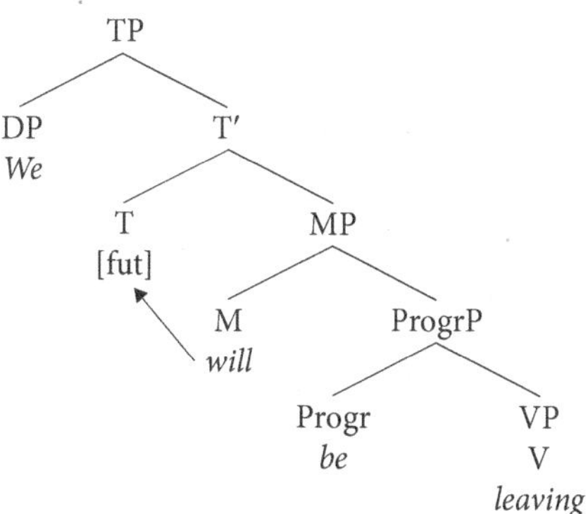

Chapter 6:   (a) Three CP-adverbials are *fortunately, frankly, hopefully* and (b) the focus presents new information, which can be provided as an answer to a *wh*-question, and the topic provides old information, which often starts the sentence.

Chapter 7:   (a) The phrase is ambiguous because the factory can be making chocolate, as in the tree on the left, or be made of chocolate, as in the one on the right.

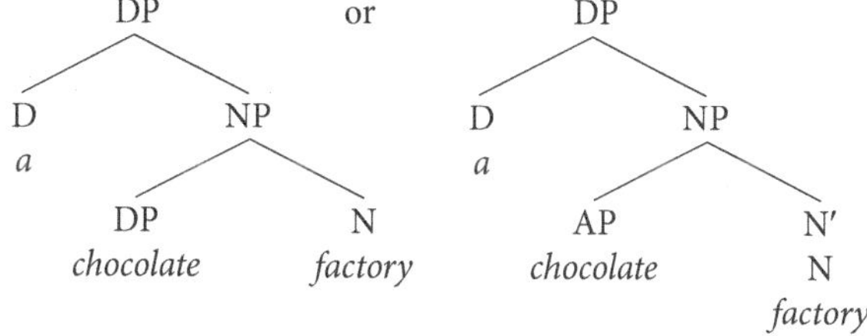

Chapter 8:   (a) Grammatical features of English are case, phi, tense, and aspect and (b) uninterpretable features do not help the interpretation, e.g. number on a verb doesn't change its basic meaning.

Index of terms and languages